UNITED STATES SENATE
OFFICE OF THE REPUBLICAN LEADER
WASHINGTON, D. C.

BOB DOLE   March 21, 1996
KANSAS

Dear Dr. Schatz:

It was recently brought to my attention
that you played an instrumental role in the
discovery of streptomycin, and I wanted to
extend my thanks and best wishes.

During my recovery after World War II,
streptomycin defeated an infection that
threatened my life.

I have long been inspired by the Kansas
State Motto--"To the stars through
difficulties." Because of your discovery, I
was able to persevere through some
difficulties, and I have every confidence that
you will persevere through yours.

If I can be of any help in the future,
please feel free to call upon me.

Best Regards,

BOB DOLE

Dr. Albert Schatz
6907 Sherman Street
Philadelphia, Pennsylvania 19119

FINDING DR. SCHATZ

FINDING DR. SCHATZ

The Discovery of Streptomycin and A Life it Saved

Inge Auerbacher and Albert Schatz

iUniverse, Inc.
New York Lincoln Shanghai

FINDING DR. SCHATZ

The Discovery of Streptomycin and A Life it Saved

iUniverse books may be ordered through booksellers or by contacting:

iUniverse
2021 Pine Lake Road, Suite 100
Lincoln, NE 68512
www.iuniverse.com
1-800-Authors (1-800-288-4677)

ISBN-13: 978-0-595-37997-2 (pbk)
ISBN-13: 978-0-595-82368-0 (ebk)
ISBN-10: 0-595-37997-4 (pbk)
ISBN-10: 0-595-82368-8 (ebk)

Printed in the United States of America

THIS BOOK IS DEDICATED

TO EVERYONE WHOSE LIFE HAS BEEN SAVED

BY STREPTOMYCIN

"Whoever saves a single life is as if one saves the entire world."

—Talmud

Contents

ACKNOWLEDGMENTS

Because Albert Schatz died before this book was completed, the following acknowledgments are by Inge Auerbacher.

My most heartfelt thanks go to Vivian and Albert Schatz for opening their hearts and souls to me.

I am grateful to Felicia Friedland Weinberg, my brilliant editor, who fine-tuned my words and made them sing.

I am most thankful to my newly adopted Schatz and Tunick cousins, the Lorraine Cande and Stanley Rosoff families; and to my new aunt, Flora Schatz-Dickman, who shared much background material with me.

I am indebted to Professor Romano Locci of the University degli Studi di Udine, Italy, for giving me permission to quote material from Albert Schatz's paper, *The True Story of the Discovery of Streptomycin*, published in the *Actinomycetes* journal, 1993.

My thanks to Steve Lipman, journalist at *The Jewish Week* in New York City, for helping to make it possible for Albert Schatz and me to meet.

Appreciation also goes to Dr. Doris Jones-Ralston; Dr. Milton Wainwright, Department of Molecular Biology, University of Sheffield, England; Dr. George Alonso, Director of Infection Control and Tuberculosis Services at City Hospital Center in

Elmhurst, New York; Mary L. Brewster for her helping hand; Professor Douglas E. Eveleigh, Cook College at Rutgers University, New Jersey, for sharing important material and making my visit to Rutgers productive; and Dr. Ross Tucker of the Mayo Clinic, Rochester, Minnesota, for sharing his thoughts.

I am also indebted to my good friend, Seymour L. Goldstein, who gave me hope, council and inspiration.

Special thanks to Lauren Simeone Berman for her creative help in bringing old photographs back to life; to Paul Weinberg for his advice and help, and to Ed Weinberg for his final sweep and excellent attention to detail.

PROLOGUE:
WHEN LIVES
INTERSECT

A cataclysm of events brings strangers together. Two individuals born oceans, continents, and years apart, come together as if by plan. Both are destined to overcome great assaults on their lives. One is a child survivor of the Nazi holocaust; the other, a retired scientist. Nothing in life happens by chance, a spiritual person would explain. There is a reason for everything.

An article in the January 24, 1997 New York City-based publication, *The Jewish Week*, caught my eye. Not because of its dramatic headline, "A Dose of God," but because I am interested in the fields of spirituality and healing. The article presented interviews of clergy and health professionals. Among them was a statement by Dr. Albert Schatz, a retired professor of Science Education at Temple University in Philadelphia.

The article noted that in 1944, while Schatz was a graduate student, he was co-discoverer of the antibiotic streptomycin.

Though it was winter, all of a sudden it felt like the 4th of July to me. I heard the blast of firecrackers and saw the blazing lights of exploding fireworks. I kept on re-reading the phrase, "co-discoverer of streptomycin."

I had been under the impression that Selman Waksman, who had received the Nobel Prize, was the *sole* discoverer of streptomycin, a drug that had twice been instrumental in saving my life. I had always wanted to get in touch with Waksman, to thank him for his great discovery and to tell him about the life that he had saved. But over the years I continually postponed my search, until I read that he had passed away.

Streptomycin became known as the "miracle drug" of the late 1940s. It was the first medicine to have any effect in the treatment of tuberculosis, a sickness that has claimed billions of lives worldwide. One of the most feared and dreaded diseases of all time, "TB," as it is known, was a disease carrying a stigma associated with the likes of leprosy.

TB was also the sickness that I contracted as I was otherwise trying to survive while incarcerated in the Nazi Terezin concentration camp in Czechoslovakia.

Tuberculosis is often called "the poor man's disease," since it is frequently a disease of slums and consequent bad nutrition. Through the years it acquired different names, like "The White Plague," or "Consumption," since it snuffed out lives with the sharpness of a knife.

I telephoned Steve Lipman, the author of the article, and pleaded with him to help me contact Albert Schatz as soon as was possible. Time was of the essence; I didn't want to follow the usual protocol of sending a letter to the newspaper, which would waste time being forwarded to the correct address.

After explaining to Lipman that Schatz had saved my life with streptomycin, and that I had no sinister motive in mind other than only to thank him, he reluctantly gave me Schatz's address. But he let me know in no uncertain words that he was breaking his publication's policy of privacy, and that he was not happy.

I wrote Schatz a letter on the same day, hoping that he would respond. Within a few days, I received a phone call.

"This is Albert Schatz, I was so happy to receive your letter."

I could barely hold back my tears. "Oh my God, oh my God, it's you!"

We had many telephone conversations during the next few months. We both felt a special bond uniting us, that of healer and patient. During our talks, bits and pieces of the discovery of streptomycin were strung together, giving me a beginning of the picture of the monumental task that the discovery had been.

Finally we set a date to meet: October 9, 1997. Early that day I took a Greyhound bus to Philadelphia, where Dr. Schatz lived with his wife, Vivian.

It was a pleasant fall day. Nevertheless, I felt unbearably warm, perhaps from anticipation. As we got closer to Philadelphia, my heart began to pound faster and faster. I felt as if it wanted to leap out of my chest, I was dizzy from excitement. So many years had passed, and now I would finally meet the man who had been responsible for saving my life. I could thank him in person for giving me such a great gift.

I barely heard the bus driver announce, "Philadelphia." I got up from my seat nervously, clutching a briefcase filled with memorabilia. All of a sudden I felt cold, as if an icy hand were touching my spine.

How would the meeting go? Would Dr. Schatz like me? Would my story be of interest to him?

Our telephone calls had been congenial. In person, "Albert," as he asked me to call him, had a surprisingly fabulous sense of humor. What could have been a disappointing meeting turned out to be the beginning of a lasting and meaningful friendship.

But I'm jumping ahead of myself. After I exited the bus, wobbly from the long ride and tense with anticipation, it didn't take long to find Dr. Schatz. He was a handsome, older man of medium height, dressed casually, with a baseball cap carelessly perched on his head. He blended in well with the crowds usually seen in bus depots.

We gravitated toward each other as if drawn by an invisible magnet.

"You are Albert," I said with awe, as we embraced each other. Both of us had tears in our eyes. It was as if at long last I had found a missing relative I had never even known I had.

We strolled to a nearby kosher Chinese restaurant not far from the bus station. Luckily it was not crowded, and we were able to talk for hours without interruption. I don't remember what we ate, we were so totally absorbed in our conversation. Time seemed to stand still as a great puzzle was unraveled. The story of streptomycin was full of surprises, betrayals, and broken promises. It had all the elements of a good detective story!

All too soon, Albert walked me back to the bus station. We found it difficult to part.

"We must meet again soon," he said. "Next time you'll come to our home and meet my wife, Vivian."

I was glad that the ride back to New York took a few hours. It gave me time to attempt to digest all the things that I had heard. Albert and I had been brought together because of the horrendous impact of a germ on my lungs. We had both experienced injustices in our lives.

Our phone conversations continued and our friendship grew. I felt increasing anger at the lack of recognition Albert had received for the important part he had played in the streptomycin saga.

Streptomycin, a drug considered one of the most important medical discoveries of the 20th century, earned a Nobel Prize for Selman Waksman in 1952. But Waksman's primary assistant, Albert Schatz, by rights should have equally shared the honors given as author of this great invention.

"The world must know the truth, Albert," I said. "You must write a book, and tell your side of the story," I implored, until finally he gave in to me.

"Fine, Inge, but let's do it together. You tell your story, you be the voice for all those who benefitted from streptomycin, and I will write my part."

I soon visited Albert again to discuss the format of our joint venture. Our meeting was at his house, where I met his lovely, charming wife, Vivian, who was as warm and generous to me as Albert was. She, too, had studied science. They appeared to be a perfectly matched couple.

How ironic it is that I, whose life had been saved by Albert, should now be involved in helping him to receive proper recognition for his greatest achievement, and a proper place in history.

Above all, we are two persons with different life stories, linked together forever—he as facilitator, and I as recipient—in our quest for a better, illness-free life.

Here's how it all started, with my letter to Dr. Schatz:

February 18, 1997

Dear Dr. Schatz:

I recently read about you in *The Jewish Week*, and found out that you are the co-discoverer of streptomycin. I contacted the reporter to get your address.

I know that you must be surprised to hear from me, and wondering who I am. Please permit me to introduce myself:

I am a child survivor of the Holocaust, and spent three years, between 7 and 10 years of age, in the Terezin concentration camp in Czechoslovakia—one of the 100 children who survived out of 15,000. I came to America in 1946, and spent my entire adult life as a chemist in diagnostic and medical research.

My memories are still very sharp, and I wrote the best-selling, award-winning children's book: *I Am A Star—Child of the Holocaust*, published originally by Simon & Schuster, and now in paperback by Penguin. It is in 8 languages, but for many survivors it was not over when it was over. The effects of these years were especially hard on a child.

I had contracted Tuberculosis of both of my lungs: spent 2 years in an American hospital with not much change in my condition. It is only after I was given streptomycin (2 times for long periods) that I finally recovered.

The Nazis robbed me of my childhood, and this awful bug took away almost my entire young adult years (close to 10 years).

Dear Dr. Schatz, I owe you my life. No words of gratitude can express the influence your discovery had on me. I am only alive today, because of this miracle drug. Because of my health background, I chose medical science as my life's work.

I have written a sequel: *Beyond the Yellow Star to America*, which deals with my tremendous battle of fighting TB, and becoming a productive human being.

I would love to meet you, if that is possible, and just put my arms around you and say: "Thank you!!"

May G-d bless you and your family.

Much love,

Inge Auerbacher

As time went by, it became apparent that Albert's health was deteriorating. There were many starts and stops to the writing of his story, and this book almost did not happen. When everything was at a standstill, Albert asked me to complete his part of the book. Since both our lives were forever bound by his co-discovery of the antibiotic streptomycin, which saved my life, we decided to tell both stories together in the same book. We both felt that this is a story too important to sink into the darkness of history.

TB's deadly history goes back to the age of the pharaohs. Not even the likes of Frederic Chopin, Robert Louis Stevenson, Vivien Leigh or John Keats were spared from its destruction.

This book tells the stories of two very different families. The Schatz family lived on the edge of poverty in America. My family enjoyed a comfortable life in Germany, until the hellish ravages of the Holocaust struck.

I am indebted to Albert Schatz to the core of my being. He generously permitted me to enter his life, via his archives and writings. I am grateful to Vivian, Albert's wife and soulmate, who made the conclusion of this journey a success.

Albert had written a great deal of his story, and I cut and pasted his remarks, thus leaving his story in his own voice. Sadly, Albert passed away on January 17, 2005, at age 84. I shall never forget this wonderful, gentle, and humorous man, the "humane" being who gave me the gift of life.

Inge Auerbacher

ALBERT SCHATZ'S STORY

THE EARLY YEARS

I was born in a hospital in Norwich, Connecticut, on February 2, 1920, the son of Rachel and Julius Schatz. My father was a Jewish immigrant from czarist Russia, which he left when he was eight years old. My mother was born in Colchester, Connecticut, to an English-Jewish farm family. My two younger sisters, Sheila and Elaine, were born in Passaic, New Jersey.

My first few years of life were spent on the family farm in Fitchville, Connecticut.

Fitchville is in a hilly, wooded area in south-central Connecticut. When the Schatz family bought the farm, the area was mostly rural and agricultural. They named their property "Bird's Eye View Farm."

My father's parents, Sam and Rose Tunick-Schatz, had 12 children, including a set of twins who died young.

My mother was a beautiful dark-haired, short and slender woman, a hard-working and loving mother. Dad was dark-haired and slender, with an athletic build. He was a little taller than my mom. Before his marriage to my mother, he played basketball and he was a light-weight boxer in his free time.

Dad met mother in Norwich, Connecticut, when he was delivering vegetables from the farm by horse and wagon. Mother was working at that time as a bookkeeper in a bakery. Dad introduced himself to her as she sat on a high stool, which was necessary to avoid the rats which brazenly scurried around on the floor of the store.

My parents had dual residences. Part of the time we lived on the farm with other members of the Schatz clan, part of the time in Norwich, not far from the farm.

It was very hard to make a living on the farm for so many members of the family. We had to supplement our income with other work, which is why we lived in two places rather than on the farm alone.

Dad and his brother, Jack, owned a paint store in Norwich. While Jack remained in the store, Dad went out to homes to paint and hang wallpaper. Mom saved half of Dad's salary each paycheck, because work as a painter was seasonal and life was financially hard during the winter months. Dad rotated his schedule between paint jobs and working on the farm, where there was always a steady supply of food to feed both his immediate and extended families.

Mom's sister married a butcher in Newton, in northern New Jersey. When the family needed more food, we would go there and come home with meat products. Sometimes we even stayed with my aunt and uncle for short visits.

I grew up on the farm during the Depression era, as part of a large extended family. We existed on what we harvested, along with proceeds from the sale of milk from our dozen cows.

Mom's constant refrain was, "Eat it up, wear it out, make it do, or do without."

My parents, Julius and Rachel Schatz.

The family farm in Fitchville, Connecticut.

LIFE ON THE FARM

Life was especially harsh on the farm during the winter. We had no electricity, no telephone, no radio, no newspaper, and no indoor bathroom. The mailbox was a quarter of a mile away. The outhouse, which had no heat, was about 100 feet from the farmhouse. We carried water from a well about 75 feet from the farmhouse. Candles and kerosine lamps provided light.

A big black iron stove, which burned wood both day and night, warmed only the kitchen. It was too cold to take baths in the winter, but in late fall and early spring, we sometimes bathed in the kitchen in a big, galvanized tub filled with pails of water which had been heated on the stove. We seldom washed clothes in the wintertime.

Our horse and wagon was of no use in deep snow; we had no tractor, so we couldn't clear the roads of snow. It was impractical to shovel snow by hand to clear the long paths from the farmhouse to the well, the outhouse, the barn and chicken coop. When we milked, we were exposed to cold winds blowing through the walls of the barn. We leaned against the cows to keep warm, and fought off sleep.

We delivered cans of milk in a horse-drawn sleigh, to a platform on a country road about three miles away. When I went on the "milk ride," I wrapped myself in a thick, heavy bear rug. Years later, the line of the Christmas song, "Oh, what fun it is to ride in a one-horse open sleigh," constantly perplexed me. How could riding in a one-horse open sleigh have been fun for anybody? It sure wasn't fun for me!

The thing I remember most about winter was being horrendously cold all the time. Our bedrooms had no heat and were dark because the window shutters were kept closed in an attempt to keep out the cold. We heated bricks, stones, and a solid clothes iron with a wooden handle, on the kitchen stove. We wrapped all of them in rags and took them to warm our feet in bed. I also slept under the bear rug that I used in the sleigh, in addition to blankets and quilts.

To minimize the number of trips to the general store, we stocked up on staples such as sugar and dried cereals. I did not know that doctors existed until I had my tonsils and adenoids removed when I was five years old. I had no store-bought toys. I made things from wood, tin cans, glass jars, string, buttons, wire, small stones, pieces of broken glass, dishes, clay, and small boxes, but I never thought of them as toys.

My responsibilities on the farm included making butter and cheese; washing dishes and pots and pans with cold water, sand, soap, and a rag; splitting firewood; and sharpening knives, axes, hatches, chisels, saws, and the five-foot long blade of the hay mower. I mended my own clothes, sewed patches on by hand, and darned my long socks. When the toe and heel areas of the socks were too worn to darn anymore, I cut the socks above the heels, sewed the ends together, and wore them as short socks.

I began my schooling in a one-room schoolhouse in Fitchville. There were no buses to take us to school, and the children did not go to school in the winter unless they were close enough to walk. Often the teacher could not get to school.

In other seasons, when weather permitted, I walked to and from school, about two miles each way. I took a short cut through the woods and across open fields, stepping on rocks to cross a brook about 18 feet wide.

The school itself had chair-desks, all the same size and screwed to the floor; a small blackboard; a well; an outhouse; a potbelly stove; a kerosene lamp; and a small room to store the firewood. There were 10 to 15 children, some of whom spoke no English. There was only one teacher, who taught reading, writing and arithmetic to all grade levels in both the elementary and secondary schools. We had to pay for our books, pads and pencils. There was no graduation ceremony; children just left when they had to.

At home, when we weren't outdoors in the barn or chicken coop, or asleep, we were all in the kitchen, because that was the only room with heat. For recreation we played checkers, chess, dominos and cards. We did not read books, magazines or newspapers, and we rarely received any mail.

I had no friends my own age. Children from school never visited me on our farm, nor did I ever visit them at their houses. I rarely even saw my cousins.

I had three friends on the farm. My uncle Lou, my father's brother, paid me a lot of attention. John Sunstrom, a Swedish farmhand, lived with us on the farm and ate at the kitchen table with us. I spent a lot of time with John, who played the piano by ear. One of the songs he repeatedly sang was "Red Wing." Later, when I learned to play the banjo and mandolin, this was the first song I played on both instruments.

My third friend was Sporty, a big black dog with the shape and looks of a collie. There was another dog, Sheppy, who was brown, white and tan, and about the size of Sporty. Of the two dogs, Sporty was my favorite. We spent a lot of time together, and sometimes Sporty slept with me.

My sister Elaine, Mom and I on the farm, about 1924.

My friend John Sunstrom, Swedish farmhand, about 1927.

IN PASSAIC AND
ON THE FARM

Dad's sister, Rebecca, and her husband, Abe, had a grocery store in Passaic, New Jersey. Abe and Rebecca pioneered the way for our relocation there when I was about three years old. At first Dad worked as an independent painter. When his brother Harry also moved to Passaic, he and Dad worked together for a short time.

We lived in a wooden three-story house with six apartments called "flats," at 381 Madison Street. Three apartments were in the back and three in the front. From our second floor apartment and porch, I could see the Memorial Park across the street.

Although most of my early school years were spent in Passaic, we continued to live both on the farm and in Passaic. When there were few paint jobs in the city, Dad would return to the farm to work.

One summer, to help us out financially, we took in boarders at the farm. A bungalow was built in the apple orchard, consisting of five single rooms. Three rooms had one window each, and the end rooms had two windows. Since we didn't have screens, mosquito nets were put up. Each room contained a bed frame, a mattress, one shelf on the wall, nails to hang clothing on, a single chair and a small table. The summer boarders brought their own bedding with them.

Every available space was used for boarders. One summer my father built a tent out of canvas and wooden poles. My parents and I slept in the tent and rented out our rooms. We also had a summer dining room for the boarders, and, eventually, an addition to the barn was built to house a dance floor and a piano.

One summer I slept on a cot in the small brooder chicken coop, which was usually used to hatch chickens. It had a sloping tin roof, one window without pane and glass, a door frame without a door, and a kerosene lamp.

THE HEIGHT OF
THE DEPRESSION

The depression was in full swing during the late 1920s and the early 1930s. It was very difficult to find any work. My father was fortunate to get employment with a paint contractor who, although he was stationed in Atlanta, Georgia, had jobs in many areas of the country. Dad became the head painter of a crew which did jobs in Colorado, New Mexico, and Washington, DC. My sisters, mother and I remained in Passaic while my father traveled all over, from job to job.

While he was in Washington, Dad and his crew were assigned to paint the White House, the Russian Embassy, and the Supreme Court building. When they painted the White House, if President Roosevelt was going to leave or come inside, all the painters had to temporarily remove themselves from the area. It was not permitted that anyone see the President being moved around in his wheelchair. No one was to know of his infirmity, and his family and staff managed to keep his paralysis from polio a well-kept secret.

When the paint job was completed at the Russian Embassy, Dad as head painter was called inside by the Russian Embassador, who personally thanked him. Dad looked him in the eyes and asked graciously, "There is something you can do for me. My wife would appreciate it very much if you might have an extra string of dried Russian mushrooms for her."

The Embassador sent someone to the kitchen, who returned promptly with a string of dried mushrooms. Mom was able to make many pots of barley mushroom soup from this wonderful gift.

While he was living in Atlanta, Dad went to night school to get a law degree. He graduated from Atlanta Law School on June 11, 1930, but unfortunately he was not able to use his degree in New Jersey, since out-of-state diplomas were not recognized. With his busy schedule, both at work and at school, I saw my father only sporadically during those years.

There was a drastic personal event for us in 1933: the barn burned down, and the entire Schatz family had to leave their homestead.

Dad was a WWI veteran. During the 1930s, veterans had to struggle to get the bonuses that were due to them. In response to this, there were Bonus Marches, and tent cities rose in Washington, DC. These tent city protests were broken up by General Eisenhower and General MacArthur.

My father finally received his veteran's bonus just before my high school graduation in 1938. He said, "Okay, son, now you can go to college!"

Consequently, I told my principal at Passaic High School, "I'm going to college!"

The principal laughed. I pointed my finger at him. "You went to college, and I'm going to go to college!"

I experienced both hard times and happiness working and living on the family farm. Despite the harsh winters and the difficult life on the farm, I wanted to become a farmer when I grew up.

COLLEGE

With the aid of a scholarship, I was able to enroll at Rutgers University in 1938, with plans of becoming a farmer after graduation. I therefore became an "Ag" (Agricultural) student at the New Brunswick, New Jersey campus of Rutgers University. Knowing very little of what the College of Agriculture was, I was overwhelmed by the size of the campus and by the number of buildings.

I lived in a dormitory during my first semester at the college. An incident occurred at that time which would have a profound influence on my life: one evening during Freshman Week, there was a knock on my door. A well-dressed and well-groomed gentleman, much shorter than I, stood in the doorway. I was in my underwear shorts.

He said, "Are you Albert Schatz? Would you mind if I ask you some questions?"

I thought that he must be a professor or other college staff member, and I invited him to come inside. He continued his questions:

"Where are you from?

"Are you majoring in Agriculture?

"Do you have any farming experience?

"How did you do in high school?"

Although I was puzzled about his identity, I answered all his questions, ending with, "May I ask who you are?"

To my amazement, he answered, "I am a freshman, and I'm going to be top man in this class. I just wanted to know what competition I have."

Surprised by his answer, I responded, "Over my dead body will you be number one."

I later learned his identity, and it was not he, but I, who eventually graduated at the top of our class. Had this incident not occurred, perhaps my life would have followed a different destiny. But I was deeply challenged by his statement.

In my freshman year, I took Professor Jacob Joffe's course in pedology, the science of the origin, formation and distribution of soil. The lectures, which were related to practical farming, made great sense to me, and I consequently wanted to become a pedologist.

I also took Professor Frank Helyar's "Introduction to Agriculture." Professor Helyar was Director of Resident Instruction at the "Ag" school. He had spent his early years on a farm in New Hampshire, and he and I would often discuss farm life in New England, especially recalling the severe winters.

During the summer of my sophomore year, I worked on a farm in Connecticut, not far from where I had spent my early years. One day in late August, I returned home to Passaic, New Jersey, without calling ahead. I wanted to surprise my mother.

Although she didn't hear me come in the back door, she greeted me from the front room before I had a chance to say anything. She knew I was there because she had smelled the cow manure on my shoes.

In May, 1942, I graduated from Rutgers University at the top of my class, with a major in Soil Science. The day after I received my Bachelor of Science degree, I became a student again. But this time I was a graduate student with plans to earn my Ph.D. degree.

All this schooling was very new to my family. My mother did not go to high school, but went instead to work in the bakery. My Uncle Joe, my mother's brother, who worked for a while as a painter with my father, worked in a butcher shop and later in a mattress factory to earn enough money to enroll in the University of Maryland Dental School.

My parents and my Uncle Joe considered my going to college to be an outstanding accomplishment for our family. When I first entered Rutgers, I didn't know that there was such a thing as graduate work. And when I decided to continue my studies for a Ph.D. degree, I cannot adequately express how in awe my parents and my Uncle Joe felt. We just did not know anyone who had such an advanced degree of learning.

I wanted to continue my graduate work in pedology, but Professor Jacob Joffe had no funds to offer me. Because of my academic standing in my class, I was, however, accepted by Professor Selman Waksman, to begin my Ph.D. studies in his prestigious Department of Soil Microbiology.

I worked for six months on the production of fumaric acid and three antibiotics, actinomycin, clavacin, and streptothricin. Unfortunately, these antibiotics were too toxic to have practical value in treating human infectious diseases.

After the discovery and usefulness of the antibiotic penicillin, the first antibiotic used successfully in the treatment of human suffering from various diseases like pneumonia, diphtheria and anthrax, Waksman decided to spearhead programs to find new antibiotics.

At first I was not interested in this field, but gradually the work gave me an introduction to the new horizon of miracle drugs, the world of antibiotics.

WORLD WAR II

World War II interrupted the lives of many students. In November, 1942, I became a bacteriologist in the Medical Detachment of the Air Force, and was stationed in the Army hospitals in Florida. This experience provided me with first-hand knowledge of the inability at that time to control many infectious diseases. Sulfa drugs were useful in some cases, but had serious limitations. The antibiotics tyrothricin, gramicidin and tyrocidin could be applied topically (on the skin), but were too toxic for systemic (internal) use. Penicillin was a new antibiotic discovered in England, but it was active only against gram-positive bacteria.

As a bacteriologist in the army hospitals, I personally saw the tragedy of uncontrollable gram-negative bacteria. They were killing wounded servicemen, some from the North-African campaign who had been flown back to the United States for treatment. The most common gram-negative infections were meningitis, typhoid fever and gonorrhea. Some of the soldiers with these infections died.

My actual job was to go to the bedsides of the sick soldiers and take throat smears or blood samples. I would then isolate and identify the deadly bacteria. That was the easy part.

I often spent off-duty hours with the servicemen who lay dying. They just wanted to talk to a person of their own age, to have someone listen to them. I listened carefully, though it was very painful to see young men my own age who were dying from the miserable infections. This is when and why I became deeply interested in antibiotics.

Since there was no way of effectively controlling tuberculosis and other infections caused by gram-negative bacteria, I began devoting my spare off-duty time to searching for an antibiotic that would be effective against gram-negative bacteria. For this purpose, I isolated and tested molds and actinomycetes (thread-like bacteria) from contaminated blood culture plates and from Florida soils, swamps and coastal sea water.

I knew how to do such work because I had taken a course in soil microbiology in my junior year at Rutgers. The laboratory work in that course included the procedure for isolating the soil microbes which produced antibiotics.

I sent Waksman, at Rutgers University, cultures that I thought merited further testing, which I could not do with the less sophisticated equipment in the army hospitals. Waksman later acknowledged, in a scientific publication which he co-authored with graduate student Elizabeth Bugie at Rutgers, that one culture that they had tested "…was isolated from a meningococcus blood agar plate by Private A. Schatz while he was stationed at the Miami Beach Military Hospital in April of 1943."

My research in the army was terminated when, due to a back injury, I was discharged on June 15, 1943.

I could have gotten a well-paying job in a chemical or pharmaceutical company. Instead, I chose to return to Rutgers to pursue my studies for a Ph.D. degree, which gave a college stipend of only $40 a month. I informed Waksman that for my doctoral research project I wanted to continue my search for an antibiotic against gram-negative bacteria.

Waksman agreed to my proposal. He knew that this would be a continuation of the work I had been doing during my off-duty hours at the army hospitals.

I was 23 years old and skinny, weighing only 120 pounds. I subsequently learned that at that time my stipend was the lowest of all graduate students in Waksman's department.

RETURN TO
RUTGERS

When I was a graduate student, to keep body and soul together, I lived rent-free in a small room in one of the Plant Physiology greenhouses. In return, I prepared mineral solutions for research in hydroponics (growing plants in chemical solutions without soil). I watered and fertilized other plants growing in soil, swept the floor of the workroom area, maintained the proper temperature during the winter months, and performed many other necessary chores. I ate fruit, vegetables and dairy products which I obtained free from the respective departments at the Agricultural Experiment Station.

I went home to Passaic, New Jersey, every weekend; first, because I liked to be with my family; and second, because of my meager earnings and food handouts from the different departments, I was not eating very well. At home my mom fed me beautifully and always gave me food to take back, to supplement the sparse fare I had at Rutgers.

Waksman and I had a cordial relationship. My fellow students and I looked up to him because of his pioneering work and his academic stature in Soil Microbiology. He was our mentor, a man we thought of as having the highest integrity. To us he was a God-like figure, a person we almost worshiped. He was of medium height, had dark hair, and possessed a relentless determination and curiosity in scientific experimentation. And, like myself, he was also of Russian-Jewish heritage.

Shortly after my return to Rutgers, Dr. William Feldman, a doctor of Veterinary Medicine at the Mayo Clinic in Rochester, Minnesota, visited Waksman. He suggested that Waksman look for an antibiotic to treat human tuberculosis. However, Waksman was reluctant to take on the project because, he told me, he was afraid to have mycobacterium tuberculosis, which causes human tuberculosis (TB), in his laboratory.

When I told him that I wanted to work with that organism, and include the search for an antibiotic against tuberculosis as part of my Ph.D. research, Waksman informed Feldman that he would take on the TB project. I then had two problems to work on: finding an antibiotic active against gram-negative bacteria, and an antibiotic against the tubercle bacillus.

I was extremely interested in tuberculosis, because as a young boy in Passaic, I had known children at school and also neighbors who suffered miserably from this most dreaded contagious disease. They could not afford the only unreliable and questionable treatment available at that time, which was to go to a sanatorium for complete rest, safely separated from healthy family members and friends for long amounts of time.

Without any treatment, the poor people continued to cough, which spread the lethal organism through the air and infected others. I saw them lose weight and waste away from their tuberculosis, which was more commonly called consumption.

When I was about five years old, I recall looking down from the porch of our second floor flat, which faced the street, and seeing a black wooden hearse being pulled by two black horses. A woman, whose husband had died from consumption, was crying hysterically as she was being held by family members and friends. Suddenly she broke loose, ran to the hearse, and tried to open the two vertical black wooden doors. Her friends caught up with her before she succeeded, and supported her bowed body as they led her away.

Waksman initially thought that there was little likelihood of my finding an antibiotic that would be effective in treating TB, because of the external waxy coating which protected the tubercle bacillus. He also knew that millions of tubercle bacilli got into the soil from the feces of diseased cows, and would not lose their virulence for many years to come.

Waksman had three laboratories. His office and two laboratories were on the third floor of what he called the "Administration Building." The third laboratory was in the basement of the same building. Waksman assigned me to work in the basement laboratory, because he wanted to be as far away from the tubercle bacillus as he could be. He was deathly afraid of catching the disease. That is why he never once visited me in the basement laboratory during the entire time of my research.

THE DISCOVERY OF STREPTOMYCIN

I put my heart and soul into my work as if I were on fire, testing hundreds of different colonies of "actinomycetes." Rising before sunrise and often working long past midnight, I prepared my own media and sterilized the glassware by myself. I slept on a bench in the laboratory when I was too tired to go home, which was more often than not.

I tested and isolated anything I could find. I isolated two strains of actinomycetes, later called "Streptomyces griseus," from two separate sources. Both strains produced a new substance, which I called "streptomycin."

Streptomycin was effective against both gram-negative bacteria and the tubercle bacillus. I called one strain of S.griseus "18-16," because it was the 16th actinomycete I had isolated from a heavily manured field soil. That was the 18th soil from which I obtained actinomycetes to test for antibiotic activity.

I isolated another strain of S.griseus from a petri dish which my fellow graduate student, Doris Jones (now Doris Ralston), had streaked with a swab from a "healthy" chicken's throat.

S.griseus is an actinomycete that is widely distributed in soils. Its spores can be blown around in the air and inhaled by people and animals. The chicken had probably inhaled a spore of S.griseus.

Doris was working in the laboratory of Frederick Beaudette, a veterinarian and poultry pathologist in the Department of Poultry Science at the Rutgers University College of Agriculture and the New Jersey Agricultural Experiment Station. Doris gave me some of her petri dishes, with colonies of various microorganisms, after she had made the transfers that she wanted for her research. Having no further use for them, she passed them to me through a basement window. I called that second isolate "D-1," because it was the first (Number 1) actinomycete that I isolated from the plates that Doris ("D") gave to me.

Both strains of S.griseus arrested the growth of the most virulent strain of the tubercle bacillus, H-37, which was obtained from Dr. William Feldman of the Mayo Clinic. They also stopped the growth of some bacteria that were resistant to penicillin. Both strains of S.griseus produced streptomycin, which was effective against gram-negative bacteria and the tubercle bacillus.

I shall never forget October 19, 1943. At about 2 PM, I knew that I had discovered a new antibiotic, which I named "streptomycin." I was ecstatic! All the nights and days I had spent working to achieve this possible new cure had been worth it.

I sealed the test tube containing the agar slant with growth of S.griseus, the organism that produced streptomycin, by heating the open end and twisting the soft, hot glass. I was very happy, but also very tired. My first thought was to show my discovery to my mother.

At this point I had no idea how this new antibiotic would fare in further studies, or if it could be useful in treating humans. A battery of additional tests would now be necessary to determine its usefulness.

Waksman, for instance, already knew that the strain of S.griseus which he had isolated in 1916, and still kept in his culture collection, did not produce any antibiotic. But my discovery still remained to be proven effective to humans. I was guardedly optimistic.

Because I wanted my family to see what I was doing, I routinely took petri dishes, tubes of agar slants, cultures, and an inoculating needle to Passaic when I visited. I showed my parents and Uncle Joe how I transferred cultures, how one organism inhibited another by the cross-streak test in a petri dish, and how streptomycin inhibited the growth of bacteria. I sterilized the inoculating needle in the flame of a gas burner on the kitchen stove, and left the plates and tubes with them so that they could see how bacteria, actinomycetes, and molds grew and formed into colonies.

In the laboratory at Rutgers University, 1943.

NOTHING BUT
THE FACTS

I worked independently most of the time, since Waksman had told me that he was deathly afraid of tuberculosis, with good reason, since at that time there was no effective treatment of TB. Even bed rest and heavy exposure to the sun too often did little to slow down the assault by the bacillus on the continually weakening body. The mortality rate from tuberculosis was still extremely high. Everyone feared the "White Plague."

I insisted on working with the H-37 strain of the tubercle bacillus (the one which I had obtained from William Feldman at the Mayo Clinic), because it was the most highly virulent strain then available. Feldman advised me to be very careful with it, because what I was doing was quite dangerous.

Waksman insisted that I never bring any TB culture up to the third floor where he was located. I was the first and probably the only person who ever worked with the tubercle bacillus in one of Waksman's laboratories.

The basement laboratory in which I worked was set up for soil microbiology. Therefore it had none of the safety features of a modern TB laboratory, such as a special inoculation chamber with ultraviolet light which served as a safeguard for spreading the bacillus, or positive air pressure to circulate the laboratory air through a filter in order to avoid breathing in the deadly organism. I did not even have a special incubator for my TB cultures.

I felt good, in retrospect, because no one who had used that laboratory, and no one who worked in the entire building, contracted TB, although I myself developed a positive tuberculin reaction.

Feldman subsequently developed TB, which his doctor believed was carried by the same strain of the tubercle bacillus with which we had both been working. Ironically, Feldman's life was later saved by streptomycin, in combination with another newly developed drug. The discovery of streptomycin came just in time to benefit this great but humble man.

Waksman became interested and involved himself in my research only after I had isolated the two strains of S.griseus, which produced the new antibiotic which I had named "streptomycin." Both strains inhibited the growth of the tubercle bacillus *in vitro*.

Waksman had others in his two third-floor laboratories verify the results which I had obtained up to that time, except for the actual work I had done with the tubercle bacillus. He was too afraid to have others work with the organism in his third-floor laboratories, one of which was right next to his office.

In my basement laboratory I also produced the streptomycin which Doris Jones used in the first *in vivo* tests in chicken embryos infected with fowl typhoid at Rutgers, and which Feldman and H. Corwin Hinshaw, a physician, used for the first toxicity tests in guinea pigs infected with the tubercle bacillus at the Mayo Clinic.

Large amounts of streptomycin were needed for the animal experiments at the Mayo Clinic. I used endless numbers of one-liter Erlenmeyer flasks containing 250 milliliters of broth. I also ran two or three stills 24 hours a day, until I had enough streptomycin to satisfy Feldman's needs.

During this time, I slept on a wooden bench in the laboratory. I drew a horizontal line with a red glass-marking pencil on the flasks from which I was distilling. If I was asleep when the liquid boiled down to the red mark, the night watchman woke me up, and I added more liquid.

This was still during World War II, when rationing was in effect. I therefore recycled organic solvents that I used in sufficiently large volumes to justify recycling. I worked day and night to produce the streptomycin. Waksman did not assign anyone to help me, but the night watchman had become my ally. I believe, incidentally, that S.griseus is the first actinomycete used for large-scale industrial production.

The stills in the basement laboratory recalled to my mind a small still that I had run during the Prohibition era, where I converted grain to alcohol. At that time I was a young boy living on the family farm in Connecticut, and it was illegal to produce alcohol commercially. There were many small illegal stills such as mine, though.

****

Soon there was a buzz in Waksman's office. The first toxicity tests on animals and humans performed at the Mayo Clinic showed tremendous promise that streptomycin was effective against the tubercle bacillus.

The new discovery was publicized, and reporters came to Waksman's office. At first Waksman invited me to be present, since our relationship at the time was amicable. But his invitations soon stopped coming, and I was able to learn the news that came from the Mayo Clinic only from publications.

Waksman orchestrated all the information fed to the media. He finally took all credit that "he alone" had discovered streptomycin. He gave lectures on the subject, while the entire time I remained working alone in the basement laboratory.

There are comments in the literature that Waksman and I did not at first fully appreciate the importance of streptomycin. This may have been true for Waksman, but it certainly was not so for me. I wanted to find an antibiotic that would be effective in treating human tuberculosis. That is why, as reported in my doctoral dissertation (Schatz, 1945), I specifically worked with a virulent human strain of the tubercle bacillus.

While it is true that I did not literally point out the potential importance of streptomycin for treating tuberculosis in the paper I wrote about streptomycin inhibiting the tubercle bacillus *in vivo* (Schatz et al., 1944), there was insufficient information at that time about the toxicity and *in vivo* efficacy of the drug. I therefore did not want to raise people's hopes with claims that might subsequently be refuted.

ALL WAS NOT WORK

There was almost no time to go on dates during the stressful days and months of experimentation. In any case, I certainly could not afford to take a girl out, since my stipend of $40 a month barely covered my most essential needs. I could not afford a car, or take a girl to the movies or out to dinner. But I had my own idea of how to alleviate this misfortune. I liked to walk, and I hoped that this recreation would also be enjoyed by my dates.

One day I called a girl who had been taking walks with me. She was a student at the New Jersey College for Women (now Douglass College), which was next to the Agricultural College. She wasn't at home, and another young woman answered.

"I'll walk with you," she said.

This young woman, Vivian Rosenfeld, turned out to be my soul mate. Vivian had twinkling blue eyes and beautiful dark, curly hair that fell over her shoulders. Her smile could melt the ice caps of Alaska, and I was immediately smitten with her and with her keen sense for discovery. Vivian was also an agricultural student and so we complemented each other, although we had different specific interests in our scientific pursuits.

Vivian's parents had come to Philadelphia from the Ukraine in Russia. She had a State Scholarship, and earned $10 a week working in the bacteriology laboratory. We frequently had our "dates" in my basement laboratory. When Vivian knocked on the laboratory windows, I would go to the front door and let her in. She would do her homework while I continued with my research.

Most of our dates consisted of walking. She was a quick walker and I had a hard time keeping up with her, since the long hours I worked in the laboratory zapped my energy.

After we met, I stayed in New Brunswick most weekends, so that Vivian and I could continue taking our long walks together.

We both had a fascination for slime molds. I introduced her to them one day as we were walking in the woods uncovering decaying logs. The molds covered the woodland flora like a strange bouquet of many colors. Vivian had a fascination with wild flowers and an intense interest in nature. The slime molds brought her to a different level of discovery. We also searched together for fungi and rock lichen.

Vivian had a spring break of a week, and since she had no school, we married on March 23, 1945. Because I was in the midst of my experimentation to find strain variations of my actinomycetes cultures, I took my test tubes, covered with cotton plugs, on our honeymoon, so that I would be able to continue my observations.

Vivian and I on a date.

Vivian and I happily married, March 23, 1945.

THE PATENT
CONTROVERSY

I did not know that in 1944 Waksman had entered into a special relationship with the Merck Pharmaceutical Company, which was paying him as a consultant. Recognizing the possibility of the great financial reward for the discovery of a new antibiotic, Waksman had convinced Merck to produce streptomycin in big quantities, to be used in large-scale human trials.

At this time I was senior author of two major publications reporting the discovery of streptomycin and the ability of streptomycin to inhibit the growth of the tubercle bacillus *in vitro*. The order of authorship on the first article was: "Schatz, A., Bugie, E., and Waksman, S.A." The second paper, published in 1944, listed the order as "Schatz, A. and Waksman, S.A." I was also the senior author of a report presented at the Proceedings of the National Academy of Sciences in 1945.

It was heretofore unprecedented for a graduate student to be listed as the senior author of three publications reporting a discovery of such major importance. But Waksman knew that everybody in his department was well aware of what I had accomplished, and how hard I had worked to accomplish it. Waksman had never given the honor of first-listed authorship to anyone else prior to this.

On January 31, 1945, Waksman signed an "Oath" as part of the patent application, which read:

> Selman A. Waksman and Albert Schatz…being duly sworn, depose and say…they verily believe themselves to be the original, first and joint inventors…

Shortly after signing this oath, Waksman also signed an affidavit for a patent application, in which he referred to "'streptomycin,' the new antibiotic which Schatz and I have discovered."

Elizabeth Bugie's name was not included as part of the patent application. She was a graduate student at the time that I was doing my graduate work. She considered her involvement in the discovery of streptomycin to be minor, since she was merely delegated at times to confirm my results. Bugie, in her affidavit, referred to "streptomycin which he (Schatz) and Dr. Waksman, discovered." She also stated that she "had no part in the actual discovery of streptomycin."

This fact is very important, because many years later, after Bugie's death, her daughter claimed in the obituary that her mother should have gotten credit for her role in the discovery of streptomycin, and should have gotten more than her tiny share of royalties. The daughter stated: "She was a woman in a field of men, and she was pressured." Bugie's daughter felt that her mother had been cheated in terms of receiving proper credit and recognition for her part in the streptomycin discovery. But Bugie herself had not felt that was the case.

By July, 1945, I had earned my Ph.D. degree after two and a half years, bypassing the receipt of a master's degree. The title of my dissertation was "Streptomycin, an Antibiotic Agent Produced by Actinomycetes Griseus." It was 127 pages long. This does not include the five months I worked on the production of fumaric acid, actinomycin, clavacin and streptothricin, which had nothing to do with my research on streptomycin.

I drove myself very hard, because I knew how serious tuberculosis and gram-negative infections were, and how important it would be to find antibiotics to control those diseases. What I was working for was therefore much more meaningful to me than simply meeting the minimum requirements for a Ph.D. degree.

On May 6, 1946, Waksman asked me to sign the patent assignment to the Rutgers Research and Endowment Foundation. He had already signed it. He told me that we would each get $1, and gave a Foundation check payable to me for $1.

But Waksman did not tell me that he by himself had an agreement with the Foundation as of May 3, 1946, according to which he would receive 20% of all royalties. If Waksman had told me that he would be receiving 20% of the royalties, I would never have signed that assignment for $1.

Waksman asked me to stay on in his department after I completed my Ph.D. degree in 1945. I agreed, although my salary was only $3600 for the year, because Vivian was completing her senior year at the New Jersey College for Women at Rutgers.

The streptomycin patent was granted on September 21, 1948.

I signed away my streptomycin patent rights and royalties for three reasons:

1. I did not want poor people to have to pay large sums of money for the privilege of being able to stay alive.

2. I performed the streptomycin research at a state college. I felt that no one should get patent royalties for work supported by the government. But that "no one" included Waksman.

3. Waksman assured me, falsely, that he would not receive any royalties.

I left Rutgers in 1946 and worked in various research positions. While working at the New York State Department of Health in Albany, I started research that would lead to the discovery of nyastatin, the first drug for the cure of thrush infections. After that I worked for a year at the Sloan Kettering Institute in New York City, hoping to find an antibiotic against cancer.

But I still wanted to return to soil microbiology, so I arranged to do a post-doctoral year of study (using the G.I. Bill) at the Hopkins Marine Station, a branch of Stanford University in Pacific Grove, California.

Before we began our drive to California, I visited Waksman, who had tried to get me a fellowship from the Rutgers Endowment. Unfortunately the fellowship never materialized.

He asked, "How are you doing financially?"

I told him that we were just getting by on my small G.I. check of $90 a month.

Eventually, Waksman sent me a check for $500. I thanked him and offered to repay him. Two more checks followed, of $500 each, along with a note, "Make sure you pay income tax on it!"

We were certainly able to use the money, since Vivian was now pregnant with our first child. We lived in an old railroad shack with a leaky roof, which I tried to fix with tin cans. Vivian received $10 a week for washing laboratory glassware.

It became obvious to me that these "gifts" actually were coming from the streptomycin royalties that Waksman was receiving. I questioned him about how I should declare these sums on my income tax.

At this same time I also received letters from Waksman requesting that I sign notarized forms for streptomycin royalty assignments from Japan, New Zealand and Canada. I asked Waksman to sign a statement clarifying that he was not personally profiting from these royalties; otherwise, I would not agree to affix my signature to the forms.

I received a note from the lawyer for the Rutgers Research and Endowment Foundation stating that none of Waksman's associates had ever profited from any royalties. The message was a garbled one, and the deception became clear to me.

selman a. Waxsman

albert Schatz

OATH

STATE OF *New Jersey*   )
) : SS
COUNTY OF *Middlesex*   )

SELMAN A. WAKSMAN and ALBERT SCHATZ

the above-named petitioners, being duly sworn, depose and say that they are citizens respectively of the United States

residing respectively at New Brunswick, County of Middlesex, and State of New Jersey ; and Passaic, County of Passaic, and State of New Jersey , and that

they verily believe themselves to be the original, first and joint inventors of an improvement in

CHEMICAL COMPOUNDS AND PROCESSES FOR PREPARING THE SAME

described and claimed in the annexed specification; that they do not know and do not believe that the same was ever known or used before their invention or discovery thereof, or patented or described in any printed publication in any country before their invention or discovery thereof, or more than one year prior to this application, or in public use or on sale in the United States for more than one year prior to this application; that said invention has not been patented in any country foreign to the United States on an application filed by them or their legal representatives or assigns more than twelve months prior to this application; and that no application for patent on said improvement has been filed by them or their representatives or assigns in any country foreign to the United States.

Subscribed and sworn to before me)   *selman a. Waxsman*
this 31st day of *Jan* . 1945.)   *albert Schatz*

                        Russell Page
                        Notary Public   14

The Patent Oath, January 31, 1945.

DEPARTMENT OF COMMERCE
UNITED STATES PATENT OFFICE

To all persons to whom these presents shall come, Greeting:

THIS IS TO CERTIFY that the annexed is a true copy from the records of this
office of the File Wrapper and Contents, in the matter
of the

Letters Patent of
Selman A. Waksman and
Albert Schatz, assignors to
Rutgers Research and Endowment
Foundation,

Number 2,449,866,   Granted September 21, 1948,

for

Improvement in Streptomycin and Processes of Preparation,

IN TESTIMONY WHEREOF I have hereunto set my
hand and caused the seal of the Patent Office to be
affixed at the City of Washington, this twenty-seventh
day of   May   , in the year of our Lord
one thousand nine hundred and fifty-three
and of the Independence of the United States of
America the one hundred and seventy-seventh.

ATTEST:

J. A. Reynolds
Chief of Division.

Robert C. Watson
Commissioner of Patents.

U. S. GOVERNMENT PRINTING OFFICE   16—11386-2

The Streptomycin Patent granted to Waksman and Schatz,
September 21, 1948.

THE LAW SUIT

Much publicity was swarming around about the discovery of the new antibiotic, and Waksman appeared on the cover of *Time Magazine* on November 7, 1949, where he was proclaimed to be the sole discoverer of the new wonder drug streptomycin.

In 1949 I also learned to my dismay that Waksman had secretly been receiving royalties, contrary to his personal assurance to me that neither of us would do so. I therefore instituted a lawsuit against him and the Rutgers Research and Endowment Foundation on March 10, 1950, while we were still living in California.

I retained Jerome C. Eisenberg of Newark, New Jersey, as my lawyer. I am sure the scientific community thought me brazen, and perhaps ungrateful, for initiating such a process. But I had to live by my principles: "This above all: To thine own self be true."

Pre-trial depositions taken for that lawsuit revealed that Waksman had by that time secretly received $350,000 in royalties, although he had publicly denied receiving any royalties whatsoever.

The Rutgers Research and Endowment Foundation had received $2,600,000 in royalties. I had received no official royalties other than the few small checks from Waksman.

The lawsuit also revealed that Waksman, during the entire time I had been doing research, had a secret agreement with the Merck Pharmaceutical Company, which paid him $300 a month for consulting and for giving them exclusive information about research going on in his laboratories, along with patent rights.

The lawsuit was ugly. Waksman trivialized my work, insisting that I only followed his instructions of isolating colonies of microorganisms that he had chosen from a petri dish originally inoculated in Dr. Beaudette's laboratory at the Poultry Department of the State Agricultural Experimental Station, taken from a "sick" chicken that Doris Jones had brought to him.

Waksman had an obsession with numbers, and stated that we had tested thousands of streptomycetes for activity against TB. He further stated that I had used his 6-step procedure for my work. He credited 25 people, most of whom had very little to do with the discovery of streptomycin, including the dishwasher.

The following are some of the explanations which I presented for my defense, to counter the so-called Waksman myths:

- I worked most of the time completely independently. I prepared my own media, and washed and sterilized the glassware I used. The glass petri dishes were re-used, and test tubes were sealed with cotton plugs.

- I was the first and probably the only person who worked with the tubercle bacillus in Waksman's department, since Waksman was deathly afraid of getting sick from the bacillus. I could not possibly have isolated and tested 100,000 actino-mycetes against the tubercle bacillus in four months, which Waksman claimed to be the case.

- I did not use Waksman's so-called 6-step procedure to isolate streptomycin, but used random selection in my isolation of the two potent S.griseus strains that produced streptomycin.

- The culture that produced the D-1 S.griseus strain came from an agar plate which Doris Jones had swabbed with the contents of a "healthy" chicken's throat. She gave it directly to me after she no longer had use for the culture.

Doris Jones provided the following information: "The D-1 strain of Streptomyces griseus came from a healthy chicken's throat." She had reported that in her masters degree thesis.

"I, not Dr. Beaudette, swabbed that healthy chicken's throat. The three of us—Jones, Waksman and I, were never together at any time in Waksman's office or anywhere else. Therefore, contrary to Waksman's testimony, I was not present when he said that Jones gave him the petri dish. Waksman never saw that petri dish from which I isolated the D-1 strain of S.griseus. He therefore never told me to do anything with it. He did not select colonies, and he did not tell me to test them."

After almost a year of litigation, the suit was finally settled out of court on December 29, 1950. The royalties from strepto-mycin were to be divided in the following manner:

80% to be awarded to Rutgers. Much of this was eventually used to fund the Microbiology Research Institute that would bear Waksman's name.

10% went to Waksman.

10% was distributed to all students and others who were part of the search for antibiotics at Rutgers, including our dishwasher.

I received 3% out of the 10% and $120,000 for foreign patent rights, from which I had to pay 40% to my lawyer.

The *New York Times* featured this headline on December 30, 1950: "Dr. Schatz wins 3% of Royalty; Named Co-finder of Streptomycin."

The settlement stated: "Defendant Waksman acknowledged that 'As alleged in the complaint and agreed in the answer, the plaintiff Albert Schatz is entitled to credit legally and scientifically as co-discoverer with Dr. Selman A. Waksman of streptomycin.'"

If Waksman had denied that I was a co-discoverer of streptomycin, he would have invalidated all streptomycin patents and stopped payment on all royalties.

This settlement paved the way for future students who might discover other antibiotics or drugs to be properly compensated with royalties appropriate for their work.

THE NOBEL
PRIZE

I suppose academia was shocked and surprised that I went through with my lawsuit. How dare a David go against the Goliath of the science world—and win the case!

Needless to say, my cordial relationship with Waksman completely soured. It was hard to believe that the man I fully trusted had stolen my credit for discovery. I had never thought that such matters would happen in academia. Actions like this were possible in business, where unethical ventures are more frequent, but not in *academia.*

The perception spread that I was a litigious character, and it became very difficult to find a new position. I was disappointed that so many people did not accept the truth that was proven in the lawsuit. They folded like a cheap umbrella in a storm. Waksman was untouchable. He could do no wrong.

Academia was still under the European belief system that the professor is a God, and that as long as a student is under his wing, he or she must not make waves. Further, whatever discovery is made by a student must be credited to the department head, even if the latter's involvement had been minimal.

I was blackballed in both the science and academic worlds, because my lawsuit publicized the heretofore dirty little secret of exploitation of graduate students by professors and universities. I found myself an outcast, and I feared that the unfair stigma would follow me for the rest of my life.

I applied to more than 50 universities and research institutions, with the hopes of gaining employment. I was told that I certainly had the qualifications for the positions, but that the prospective employers were afraid of my so-called perceived litigious nature. In private, people told me, "You were right in suing Waksman, but such actions are not tolerated in academia."

I had to use a great deal of ingenuity to get a job, and I never received a position in soil microbiology again.

After I left the Hopkins Marine Station, I finally gained employment at Brooklyn College of the City University of New York. I taught bacteriology there, from 1949–1952. In 1952, I was appointed as a professor of microbiology at the Agricultural College of Bucks County, Pennsylvania.

I thought that things were finally settling down. But a new bombshell was to explode in October, 1952. The Nobel Prize for Physiology or Medicine was announced by the Caroline Institute in Sweden. It was to be awarded to Selman A. Waksman for the "Discovery of Streptomycin."

I was devastated. I thought for sure that the lawsuit had proved, beyond any doubt, my contribution to this most important discovery.

The vice president of the college in Pennsylvania where I worked wrote to the Nobel Committee on my behalf, asking them to reconsider the exclusion of my name from the award.

He included pertinent documents to substantiate his request. Former Nobel Laureates and other people in science were contacted in the effort to help me in this endeavor. But, sadly, only a few responded. Even the king of Sweden, home of the Nobel Prize, was contacted, also to no avail.

There was a lukewarm response from the Nobel Committee stating that when they researched the qualifications for the award in the United States and elsewhere, no one had mentioned my name as being the co-discoverer of streptomycin.

This was a poor excuse, since my litigation caused a great deal of publicity to be generated in the press. It is hard to believe that a prestigious publication like the *New York Times,* when it proclaimed me as the co-discoverer of streptomycin on December 30, 1950, had been overlooked, or worse yet, ignored.

The controversy must finally have opened the eyes of the Committee to the fact that there was indeed something wrong in omitting me from the prize. But although I feel that they must have seen the truth, it was too late for reconsideration. Once the formal announcement is made, there is no recourse. No revisions are permitted.

Since the Caroline Institute realized that it would be inappropriate to award the Nobel Prize to Waksman for the discovery of streptomycin, the prize was awarded to Waksman for a reason other than as the sole discoverer of streptomycin.

Thus on December 10, 1952, Professor A. Wallgren, a member of the Caroline Institute, gave that other reason in his presentation speech which was delivered before presenting Waksman with the prize. Wallgren announced:

> "Professor Selman Waksman. The Caroline Medical Institute has awarded you this year's Nobel Prize for Physiology or Medicine for your ingenious, systematic and successful studies of the soil microbes that have led to the discovery of streptomycin, the first antibiotic against tuberculosis."

The research, to which Wallgren referred, preceded the discovery of streptomycin, because that discovery was in no way dependent on the previous research.

Nobel Prizes are routinely awarded for important discoveries, not for long term research that leads to those discoveries. In awarding Waksman the Nobel Prize, the Royal Caroline Institute put the cart before the horse. The prize was not awarded to Waksman for the discovery of streptomycin, but for the long term research which led to the discovery of streptomycin. Awarding the Nobel Prize for the reason given by Wallgren violated the provisions of Statute Section 1 of the Nobel Foundation.

The following additional myths suggest that Wallgren may have gotten much of the information for his presentation speech from Waksman. Just as in the lawsuit, the following tales came up again in Wallgren's comments. I herewith want to clarify the following:

- First Myth: Wallgren stated, "…The isolation of streptomycin has been the result of…long term systematic…research." However, Wallgren himself had reduced that "long term systematic research" to a few months. Specifically, he said, "After a few months he (Schatz) isolated two strains of actinomycetes which produced streptomycin."

I was the only one of Waksman's graduate students who was mentioned by name. Waksman did not mention my name in his acceptance speech, but instead thanked, "All of my collaborators, associates, and graduate students who have participated in the investigations necessary to the development of our broad antibiotic program."

- Second Myth: Wallgren stated that the "isolation of streptomycin" was "the result of…research by a large group of workers," but I, Bugie, Waksman, were the only authors of the publication announcing the discovery of streptomycin.

As mentioned earlier, in her affidavit Bugie said, "I had no part in the actual discovery of streptomycin."

- Third Myth: Wallgren alleged that, "The initiator and leader of this group was Dr. Waksman." I did not need Waksman, or anybody, to lead me to the discovery of streptomycin.

When I was an undergraduate student in the College of Agriculture at Rutgers University, I took Waksman's graduate course in Soil Microbiology. That course included laboratory experiments in which I learned how to isolate soil actinomycetes and fungi, and how to test them for antibiotic activity.

As a graduate student, I was therefore able to work independently of Waksman and I did so, as everybody in the department knew. That is why Waksman listed me as the senior author on three papers about streptomycin, which were published while I was still a graduate student.

I wrote the original drafts of the first two papers. Waksman was vacationing at Woods Hole in Massachusetts during much of the summer of 1943, while I was working in the basement laboratory at Rutgers. Waksman was not at Rutgers many days in 1944. The only sense in which I worked *under* Waksman is that the basement laboratory, in which I worked, was *beneath* Waksman's office on the third floor.

- <u>Fourth Myth</u>: Wallgren said that streptomycin was discovered as a result of "systematic...studies." The term "systematic...studies" refers to Waksman's 6-step procedure for isolating antibiotics. However, I did not isolate the two strains of Streptomyces griseus, which both produced streptomycin, by using Waksman's 6-step procedure. I isolated the 18-16 strain of Streptomyces griseus from a heavily manured field soil.

To do that, I isolated and tested actinomycetes, which I selected at random, from a petri dish that I inoculated with highly diluted aqueous suspensions of that soil. I also isolated and tested actinomycetes selected at random from other soils selected also at random.

Doris Jones (now Ralston) was involved in my isolating the D-1 strain of Streptomyces griseus. She was working in the Department of Poultry Science in the Rutgers University College of Agriculture, a department that existed because poultry was then a major agricultural enterprise in New Jersey. As a graduate student researching the microbial flora in healthy chickens' throats, Doris's job was to smear chickens' throats with sterile swabs. She then used those swabs to inoculate an agar medium in petri dishes.

After she isolated colonies from her petri dishes for her research, she then gave me some of the petri dishes, which she would otherwise have discarded. I then isolated different colonies of actinomycetes selected at random from her petri dishes, and tested them to see whether they produced antibiotics.

I cannot understand how Wallgren could possibly have equated my selecting actinomycetes at random to what he called Waksman's "systematic...studies." Wallgren's presentation speech makes it unmistakably clear that the 1952 Nobel Prize was *not* awarded to Waksman for the discovery of streptomycin, but for studies which preceded the discovery of streptomycin. But if streptomycin had not been discovered, Waksman would not have been considered for the Nobel Prize for his research which led to the discovery of the antibiotics clavacin, fumigacin, actinomycin, and streptothricin.

In conclusion, what was Waksman's contribution to the discovery of streptomycin? He was an internationally known and highly respected soil microbiologist. I learned much about soil microbiology from him. He recognized the importance of soil microorganisms as a source of potentially useful antibiotics. The search for antibiotics was the main, but not the exclusive, focus of research in his department when I was doing my graduate work.

Am I bitter? Today there is an imposing building on the Rutgers campus in New Brunswick, New Jersey, bearing the name "The Waksman Institute of Microbiology," built largely with funds from streptomycin royalties.

On the negative side, the Nobel Museum in Sweden still continues to include wrong information about the discovery of streptomycin on its website. Waksman had three well-equipped laboratories which were available to me, even though I worked basically only in the basement laboratory. I could not have discovered streptomycin in the basement of my parent's house.

I truly hope that other students will never have to go through the agony and injustices that I endured.

On the other hand, there are many positives. I am the father of two wonderful daughters, Diane and Linda, and the grandfather of four. My precious wife, Vivian, has been my steadfast partner in all my tribulations and also travels, which eventually led to assignments in South America and different parts of the United States.

I reestablished my connection with Rutgers on April 28, 1994, on the 50th anniversary of the discovery of streptomycin. I was awarded the *Rutgers Medal*, the University's highest honor, for my work as co-discoverer of streptomycin. This honor came about largely through a 1988 publication by Professor Milton Wainwright of the University of Sheffield, England, in which my story was included.

Professor Wainwright, wanting to research the history of streptomycin, had visited Rutgers to investigate its archives. He was shocked to read about my work and my contribution to the discovery of streptomycin. He had never heard of me, and had thought that Waksman had been the sole discoverer of the important antibiotic.

His visit and findings intrigued the faculty at Rutgers, since most of them had not been on staff almost 50 years before, when the award had been presented and the consequent litigation had taken place.

Professor Wainright's conclusion was that "There can be no doubt that streptomycin was actually discovered by Albert Schatz…Anyone who reads Schatz's thesis cannot doubt that it was he who made streptomycin a reality."

Further, two test tubes of my earliest trials of streptomycin are now on display in the famous Smithsonian Institution in Washington, DC.

I have received many honors and letters from grateful patients, thanking me for saving their lives with streptomycin. But none of them touched me more than hearing from Inge Auerbacher, a child survivor of the Holocaust, who told me how I had saved her life by my discovery of streptomycin.

I have come full circle. How can I be bitter?

RUTGERS MEDAL

THE STATE UNIVERSITY OF NEW JERSEY
RUTGERS

AWARDED TO

ALBERT ISRAEL SCHATZ

As a descendant of emigrant farming parents from Czarist Russia, you expressed an early interest in agriculture and soil microbiology. These interests brought you to the College of Agriculture of Rutgers University where you earned your Bachelor of Science degree in soil chemistry, followed by the Doctor of Philosophy degree in soil microbiology after studying under the direction of Professor Selman A. Waksman, another emigrant of Czarist Russia. It was during this latter period, in 1944, that you became the co-discoverer of the important antibiotic, streptomycin, the first useful chemotherapeutic substance for the treatment of the "Great White Plague," or tuberculosis. This great discovery was made possible, in part, by your courageous use of virulent pathogenic cultures of Mycobacterium tuberculosis in your bioassay procedures. The isolation of the special strain of Streptomyces griseus that produced streptomycin, followed by its isolation and purification, led to the discovery of its in vivo efficacy against tuberculosis. The worldwide impact of this discovery is now part of medical history. Many institutions and countries have recognized the importance of your discovery and bestowed upon you awards, medals, prizes and honorary degrees. You, thus, have brought distinction and honor to Rutgers, The State University of New Jersey.

By virtue of my office as President of Rutgers, The State University of New Jersey and with deep personal appreciation of your service to mankind, I am pleased to present you the Rutgers University Award for which this medal is the symbol.

Francis L. Lawrence
Francis L. Lawrence
President

Conferred at the
Occasion of the 50th Anniversary of the Discovery of Streptomycin at
Rutgers, The State University of New Jersey
April 28, 1994

The Rutgers Medal, awarded to Albert Israel Schatz, April 28, 1994.

INGE
AUERBACHER'S
STORY

BEGINNINGS

"Berthold, please turn off the radio!" Mama pleaded. "I can't stand that loud voice. I've been feeling bad all day, and the shouting makes me feel even worse."

Mama was referring to the new German Chancellor, Adolf Hitler, who had recently come into power. The voice continued to thunder.

"Berthold, did you hear me?" And with that, Papa turned off the large brown box. The room was suddenly silent. One could almost hear the walls and the furniture in the dining room sigh with relief.

Papa did not like to take orders from anyone. But this was one time he had to give in, though reluctantly, because Mama was pregnant with their first child. He knew that she was having a hard time, but subconsciously he felt cheated because he was curious to hear what the new Chancellor had to say.

"He's just an idiot, believe me, Rina. Not many people will accept him, he'll be gone soon. He talks such nonsense. The intelligensia will surely be smart enough not to accept him. After all, this is Germany, not one of those uncivilized countries."

Papa had no patience for anything complicated. "I'll call you Rina, if you don't mind. Regina sounds too sophisticated," he had told her after their wedding on August 30, 1931.

Now it was the fall of 1934. Papa placed his hand on Mama's pregnant stomach.

"I can feel it kicking. I wonder what it will be. We'd better start thinking of names."

They invited some friends to visit, and made a game out of the baby naming. Papa took the lead and announced, "We better not choose a biblical name, just to be on the safe side. We don't want to make the baby conspicuously Jewish. It will have to be a real German name.

Names like Solomon, Samuel, Esther, or Sara belonged to another time. One by one, each friend wrote a suggestion on a small piece of paper, folded it, and dropped it into a hat. The so-called ballots were counted, and the tally was unanimous.

"If it's a girl," Papa said, "her name will be Inge," which was a very popular German girl's name at the time.

Without paying attention to the choices of boys' names, Papa continued, "And if it is a boy, he will be called Rolf."

Papa looked into Mama's grey eyes. "Do you agree, Rina?"

To the astonishment of the guests, who felt cheated, Mama nodded her approval, even though the deal was to abide by the ballot count. Yes, Rolf was one of the choices, but other names had more votes.

"Why did she have to give in so easily?" their friends wondered. They concluded, "Oh, well, it's their baby, and ultimately as the new parents they should make the final choice."

Papa was a stocky man, close to six feet tall, with a strong personality. He was quite an imposing figure. Mama, a head shorter, possessed a calmer personality. Mama almost always surrendered to Papa's wishes.

They had been married more than three years, and Mama had experienced Papa's hot temper and short fuse on many occasions. He apologized each time, saying, "It's my Auerbacher temperament!"

Giving in to his tirades was the only answer in order to have *Sholem Bayith* (a Hebrew phrase meaning, "Peace in the Home"). *Sholom Bayith* had been ingrained in her by her religious parents, who stressed that one should do everything to have a warm and peaceful home.

In her heart, Mama had wished for a girl. She did not want her baby to have to go through the ordeal of circumcision—a custom practiced by Jews for thousands of years, dating back to Abraham and the Covenant with God—which every Jewish male baby must go through eight days after birth.

Mama had a difficult pregnancy. She was sick almost every day. Their Jewish friends warned my parents, "How can you bring a child into the world at this time? Don't you know what is going on in Germany today? You are foolhardy; who knows how this will end? We see a bleak future for Jewish people in Germany."

They had been listening to the vile propaganda blasting through the airwaves: "We will treat the Jews like flowers. But we will not give them water!"

To this, Papa always answered, "I am a disabled veteran of World War I. Here, look at my Iron Cross!"

Papa would always bear scars from shrapnel that had torn into his right shoulder during the war. He would never again be able to raise his right arm properly, due to his wounds.

"They would not dare touch a good law-abiding German like me," he continued. "Don't be silly, those are the words of a bunch of hooligans. We have nothing to fear. This new baby will grow up to be a proud German, like me and my ancestors."

To this his friends always answered, "We hope you are right, Berthold, but we are not as certain of the outcome as you are."

Papa's family had lived in Kippenheim, a village at the foot of the Black Forest located in south-western Germany in the province of Baden, for at least 200 years. Kippenheim had a population of 2000, composed of about 60 Jewish families and approximately 450 Catholic and Protestant families, all living peacefully together.

Mama was born in Jebenhausen in the Province of Wuerttemberg, in an even smaller village than Kippenheim, about 200 miles away. Mama's father was a cattle dealer. Papa's father was also a cattle dealer, who also sold skins and hides. This occupation was one that was practiced by many Jews in southern Germany.

The Auerbachers, as well as Mama's family, the Lauchheimers, practiced Judaism in the modern orthodox tradition. Papa, a textile merchant, had no desire to continue in his father's skin and hide business. He preferred to work with clean hands, rather than to handle the piles of ill-smelling salted cattle hides.

Many of the Christians of Kippenheim were farmers, while the Jews in general owned small shops or were in the cattle business. Christians and Jews lived side-by-side, and had good relations with each other. Anti-Semitism reared its ugly head only on rare occasions.

Christians went to church on Sunday, while the Jews celebrated their Sabbath on Saturday. The different celebrations of their holidays did not bring clashes between the people; rather, they added to the mosaic of village life. Jews were linked with non-Jews in their patriotism and passion for Germany, and fought side-by-side in the wars, defending and dying for their country. And yet, for the most part, the Jewish community isolated itself.

My parents moved into the large house that Papa's family had owned for many years. Papa was one of six children, four sisters and an older, deceased brother, Semi. Three of his sisters, Klara, Paula and Hilde, were married and lived some distance away. Rosel, the youngest sibling, was unmarried, and therefore had inherited the house from Papa's parents who had passed away before Papa's marriage to Mama. My parents purchased the house from Rosel with the funds from Mama's dowry. The money from my parents was to be used to provide a dowry for Rosel's forthcoming marriage to a Frenchman.

Mama's only sibling, her younger unmarried brother, Karl, still lived in her family's home in Jebenhausen.

My parents had been introduced to each other through members of their respective families. Papa proposed to Mama within a few hours of meeting her.

Both Mama and Papa hired private investigators to screen each other, which was a common custom practiced by some people. The information gathered was favorable for both, and the chemistry was good between them. Papa was determined to marry his dark blond young lady, who came from a middle class background similar to his.

Mama, for her part, was enchanted by Papa's stature, dark brown sparkling eyes, his broad smile, and his large black Adler car. She was impressed that Papa was a textile merchant, not a common cattle dealer, a profession she did not want for her future husband.

Their marriage followed after only six weeks of courtship, a courtship which had been conducted mainly through frequent exchange of letters.

Now, three years later, even though many of the village women opted for childbirth in the hospital located in a nearby larger town, it was decided that Mama should have the baby at home, just like the other members of the family had been doing for generations. Kippenheim's small hospital had by this time just about closed its doors.

It became apparent that Mama's delivery would not be performed solely by the village midwife. Dr. Bernhard Weber, Kippenheim's doctor, was enlisted to help early in the pregnancy, due to Mama's pre-birth health complications. Her constant nausea, for instance, continued for the entire nine months of her pregnancy. People thought that the high-risk pregnancy was a signal, perhaps even an omen, that this child should not be born into the world of turbulence that was rapidly starting to surround them. All of Germany by this time was overshadowed by storm clouds gathering on the horizon.

But, despite health contraindications, Mama was resolved to have her baby. The baby was strong, in spite of everything, and tenaciously held on in the womb, apparently determined to see the light of day.

Dr. Weber sometimes came to Mama's bedside dressed in a Nazi uniform. He had joined the Nazi Party, but still took care of his Jewish patients. Mama was especially disturbed by this. She complained, "I don't like this uniform. I don't want my child to grow up in an atmosphere of hate. I want my child to grow up in peace."

Papa was not bothered by the doctor's uniform. He, too, had worn a uniform in World War I, and he was proud that he had fought for Germany against its enemies. But when he was deep in thought, flashes of reality managed to pierce through his brain. "These uniforms are different."

"Times are changing," he countered his other thoughts.

"But," he concluded, "I am an optimist. I am not going to let the voices of gloom and doom rob me of my joy in becoming a father."

Liesa, our live-in-maid, helped to take care of our large house. One day she heard my mother's voice calling to her frantically, "The pains are starting. Call Dr. Weber. Please hurry!"

Papa was away on a business trip, selling his sheets, pillow cases and other items to the inns that were dotted throughout the Black Forest. He would not be home until the evening. And Mama had had these symptoms before. Each time Dr. Weber proclaimed, "False alarm!"

But this time it was different. The pains were stronger and lasted longer. Mama was glad when she heard a car entering the courtyard of the house. It was Papa. He had come home earlier than expected. Liesa ran to him quickly, telling him to come to Mama's bedside.

The pains continued for 24 hours. Finally, Dr. Weber decided that Mama had gone through enough. Since the baby was now overdue, he was going to help nature take its course. Mama was placed on a table which was brought into the master bedroom on the second floor, and was given a mild anesthesia.

During the commotion, distant cousins Emilie and Max Auerbacher came to pay a surprise visit. They were quickly drawn into the goings on in the upstairs bedroom.

Dr. Weber, not shy with words, said, "Don't just stand there and watch. You can help me."

So they held Mama's legs as Dr. Weber took his forceps and pulled out the bloody baby. Papa watched from a safe distance. He was too squeamish to watch the proceedings from up close.

Dr. Weber looked over at Papa. "Herr Auerbacher, I have only a princess for you." He thought that Papa would have preferred a son who would carry on the family name.

"That's fine," answered Papa, relieved that the long ordeal was finally over.

Dr. Weber gave the baby a slap on her behind, and she let out a loud yell. "She has strong lungs," Dr. Weber commented.

He looked at his watch. It was 12:45 AM on December 31.

"Herr Auerbacher, you end 1934 with a new addition to your family. Your daughter can always celebrate *Silvester* (New Year's Eve) on her birthday."

Mama soon awakened. Even in her twilight sleep, she knew that she had given birth to a girl.

"I want to see my Ingele." She cradled her baby, counting five fingers on each hand and five toes on each foot.

"Perfect," she boasted. "And she is so big, just look at that black curly hair on her head. That was what must have given me heartburn! I was so sick all the time. I'm so glad we both made it."

She fell asleep once again, holding me lovingly in her arms.

My hometown, Kippenheim.

Our house in Kippenheim (middle).

My parents, Regina and Berthold Auerbacher.

Dr. Bernhard Weber.

MY EARLY YEARS

Papa proudly placed his Leica camera on a tripod, pushed the self-timer, and quickly ran to get into the picture. He was standing next to Frau Ketterer, our cleaning woman, and Liesa, the maid, in front of a large tub piled high with my first laundry.

He wondered, *Would they have another chance for a boy to keep up the family name?* Rina had had such a hard time, and he didn't want to jeopardize her life again. *Only time will tell,* he realized.

Papa was a religious man. He thought of the Hebrew saying, *Gamsele tovo* (everything works out for the best).

"For now I am very happy with my princess," he said, "And thank God Rina is okay!"

I was the last Jewish child born in Kippenheim. In 1935, Jewish and Christian mothers attended the same afternoon parenting classes in the doctor's office. During one of these visits, Dr. Weber chose me from a bunch of screaming babies.

"Look at this one; this is how a healthy baby should look. Not too fat, not too skinny, and very alert."

Mama was proud that I was selected. "Even if I had to go through so much with my pregnancy, it was all worth it!"

My experience in kindergarten was short-lived; Papa had to take me home after only a few hours. I raced into his arms, clinging to him as if my life depended on it. Tears ran in parallel rivers down my face as I sobbed in loud wails.

The teacher must have been happy that I was removed, since I was being such a nuisance. They knew that if one child cried, all the others would also chime in. I had not been mistreated by the Christian teacher or children, but the separation from home had been too much for me. I was much happier playing in my sandbox in the courtyard of our house, surrounded by my favorite toys, my doll, Marlene, in her light green carriage, and my teddy bear.

It was different when I visited my maternal grandparents in Jebenhausen; there I was never homesick. Jebenhausen was half the size of Kippenheim. My grandparents were the last Jewish family living there, in a village which at one time had been 40% Jewish. Most of the Jewish inhabitants had moved to the bigger cities or to America at the end of the 19th century, places where they sought better opportunities in commerce and in education.

I loved being with the cows at Opa's (grandfather's) place. They were soft and warm, and docile most of the time. It was a special treat when he allowed me to ride on them.

The stable was part of the house, separated from the main entrance. I didn't even mind the strong smell of cow manure which permeated the stable.

Oma (grandmother) let me help her feed her small chicken flock and chase them into the shed in the back of the house at night. I also helped her pick vegetables in her small garden near the house. The chickens and the vegetables were used to make chicken soup for the Sabbath and for other holidays.

I was my grandparents' only grandchild. My parents brought me to Jebenhausen on many occasions, and often left me there for a few days, or sometimes a week. I loved the long car ride in Papa's shiny black car. It was great fun to look out the window and watch the different towns whiz by.

In Kippenheim, I had only Jewish friends. My playmates were mostly boys, all older than I. I was therefore often left playing games by myself; but since we had a maid who performed most of the household chores, Mama was able to spend a great deal of time with me.

I was very happy in Jebenhausen, where I had an army of children my own age to play with. They were all Christian, but they did not show any animosity toward me, they made me feel quite at home.

We loved to take off our shoes and run across the fields, which bloomed with a bright patchwork of wild flowers. We liked feeling the cool grass squish beneath our feet during the hot summer days, as we lazily watched the birds flying above our heads. We wished that we could join them as they soared to strange and distant lands.

There was a beautiful tranquility here in these meadows. We felt like rulers of the world. In our kingdom of children and fantasy, there were no signs of bloodshed or of an oncoming war. For us, peace and the innocence of children playing was the rule. Here there was no bigotry, here no one could hurt us; no one would dare to stop our laughter, our songs, or dampen our free spirits. We created our own family in the meadows, devoid of the pressures of opinionated adults.

I was content in my grandparents' home. Oma and Opa were more permissive than my parents. Papa was a stern disciplinarian, and he possessed a loose hand. He had only to look at me with his large dark brown eyes, and even from across the room I could sense a warning and would cringe before it. It was a signal that my behavior was not proper, that I was doing something wrong, and it almost always ended with a slap on my behind. Mama often interfered on my behalf against Papa, but I was still cautious lest I arouse his wrath.

But there was also a warm side to Papa. After his outbursts he often felt sorry for his harsh actions, and would buy me a delicious pastry. The sticky, creamy sweet confection always did the trick of soothing my bruised pride as well as my physical pain. My flood of tears stopped immediately with the first bite of my treat. All was forgotten until the next episode.

I remember watching with awe as Opa wound the tefillin (special leather binders used by Jews in worship) around his left arm, before he said his morning prayers. There was also a strange looking small black leather box attached to the leather strap, which he bound around his forehead.

It was at such times, when Opa was deeply absorbed in prayer, that Oma would beg me to ask him for money.

He would always answer, "Ey, ey," meaning, "Don't disturb me now," and then he would point to his jacket pocket. I would quickly take out a few marks, and run into the kitchen, where Oma was busy with her cooking chores. It must be urgent, I thought, she probably needs the money to buy a special ingredient to add to a recipe.

Opa loved taking me for walks. His grey cat would some-times follow us. I was impatient with Opa's slow pace, caused by worsening heart problems, and I would tear loose and run ahead of him.

Each time he told Oma, "I can't keep up with the child, she walks too fast for me." But every morning he would forget the previous day's misadventure, and would again request Oma to get me ready for our outing.

I loved playing cards with Opa. I pretended to know the rules of a game called "66." Opa went along with my demon-strative boasting, and would always let me win.

Oma was hard of hearing, and we had to talk loudly for her to understand us. Her hearing aid did not work very well. And I remember her forever looking for her eyeglasses. They would always be somewhere in a pile of flour...When she was engrossed in the task of baking her challes (Jewish holiday breads) and other delicacies, they would somehow fall off and become coated in flour.

When rainstorms threatened, Oma always placed a prayer book and her house keys on the table. She never forgot the time when her large family's house was struck by lightning and burned to the ground. She wanted to be prepared in case the same thing happened again.

Oma was one of 14 children. Oma and Opa were first cous-ins. They were two of the kindest people I would ever meet in my life.

Frau Ketterer, Papa, and Liesa—my first laundry, 1935.

Inge, her parents, and grandparents in Kippenheim, 1938.

VILLAGE LIFE

Mama was happy. She felt at home in Kippenheim, where her genuine warmth, spirit and youth found special welcome in the Jewish community. It was as if a window had been opened after a long winter, letting in the fresh air of spring. Mama was embraced by the sisterhood of the synagogue, and bonded immediately with its members. She found acceptance even in the male-driven society.

Male chauvinism was felt not only in the Jewish community, but also in the gentile-German world. It was accepted that the man was the head of the home. The role of women was limited to the care of children and the household.

But Mama worked quietly behind the scenes, using her intelligence and peace-making abilities. She influenced much of Papa's decision making, although he almost always took credit for the outcome of the situation.

His loose tongue sometimes got him into arguments with other people. Mama would be asked to smooth things out and to settle disputes peacefully. She was popular with both the female and male congregants, who had great respect for her.

"Berthold is a lucky man to have married a woman like Rina," they quietly said to each other.

The center of Jewish life was the synagogue. Most of the Jewish people of Kippenheim attended Sabbath services on Saturday mornings and on holidays. It was hard to keep a secret in such a small community; the Jewish population was close-knit, and everyone knew each other's family history, including any skeletons in the closet. There could be no secrets. Everything was public domain.

There was finger-pointing when a person did not show up for worship: "Why is so-and-so not here, what is the reason?" Tongues wagged, and rumors became tall tales, often unfounded. "Ha, she is finally pregnant!" was a popular guess.

Being the youngest member of the congregation, I used this to my advantage. I was able to get away with almost anything. Many times I left my mother's side in the women's section on the balcony and snuck down to the main sanctuary where I sat next to my father in the men's section. Separation of sexes is mandated in orthodox Jewish worship.

When I was sitting with the men, Max, a distant cousin, often instigated me to cause problems. He would point to the bright chandeliers hanging over our heads like halos.

"See the beautiful lights!" he whispered to me, hoping I would respond. To his joy, I usually repeated his statement loudly. And of course my chatter disrupted the mood and solemnity of the prayers.

The parishioners immediately hissed, putting their fingers to their mouths. "Quiet! You must be respectful!"

I felt so ashamed, I wanted to cry. Reaching for the safety of my father's arms and body, I buried myself, trying to disappear.

Papa gave Max one of his threatening looks, and told him to stop his mischief. "Leave the child alone, she is so young. Don't you have something better to do? Continue your praying!"

There was always a festive spirit during our holidays. Congregants came dressed in their finest clothing. New outfits were bought for special holidays like Rosh Hashanah, the Jewish New Year. I remember my Sabbath dress, maroon velvet with a white collar, that was sewn especially for me. The outfit was completed with a white hat that covered my thick black curly head of hair. My parents would proudly parade me in front of the other congregants.

Mama made sure that I was brought up with a good dose of religion. She would sit next to me on my bed every night and listen to me say my prayers. She taught me the proper Hebrew ones, and I was encouraged to add in German my own version of wishes and special messages to God.

It was common practice to visit one another after worship, and to invite strangers into our homes for dinner.

I especially remember the visits of Mr. Nissensohn, a poor Jewish man from Poland. He sold buttons and thread to the Kippenheim populace—mostly to the Jewish population, who bought from him mainly out of pity rather than of necessity.

Our meals were probably the only good food he had all week. We usually had chicken noodle soup, followed by short ribs of beef, potato, and lettuce salad. Mr. Nissensohn ate with appreciation and with great appetite.

STORM CLOUDS

National socialism or Nazism in Germany was taking deeper roots every day during the late 1930s. It was felt even in the smallest villages, and was slowly creeping into many phases of German life. Special sporting events for Aryans only were advertised on large posters. The sounds of new infectious marching songs, peppered with German nationalistic lyrics, were heard on the radio and sung at special events. The catchy tunes often contained hateful words against the Jews. They were sung widely by many Germans.

The sudden change of behavior brought shock and outrage to some Jews, but most listened with deaf ears. Such outrage was impossible in their beloved Germany, they said as they shrugged off the foreboding signs.

Germany had been a seemingly safe place for Jews for hundreds of years. In general, Jews lived assimilated lives in their new homeland, and had always assumed that they were equal citizens with the Gentile populace.

Many German Jews were anesthetized with the ether of arrogance, believing that they were untouchable. They were not like their Jewish brothers and sisters in Eastern Europe, whom they felt never wanted to blend into the cultures of their respective countries. It was rare to see Jews in Germany wearing the signs of Eastern European orthodoxy, beards and strange black outfits and earlocks which were worn by religious men and young boys. The Jews of Germany felt that was why Jews elsewhere were having problems. They were drawing too much attention to themselves, and stood out too much.

Germany had been defeated in World War I, and left humiliated. Depression in spirit and economy enveloped the country. Adolf Hitler seized the opportunity to promise Germany the seemingly impossible: to make it a great power once again, and to solve all its problems.

Germany embraced the charismatic Austrian-born failed artist with open arms. His continued spewing of venom against the Jews did not bother most of the people, who willingly accepted the scape-goating as an answer to all their woes.

Large boisterous meetings in beer halls and auditoriums generated much excitement. It was as if Germany were on fire, fanned by the flames of hatred against enemies of the new Nazi party, but especially fanned against the Jews.

The newly composed song containing the lyric, "When Jewish blood drips from the knife, it tastes twice as good," was sung with great spirit by marchers in the perpetually-held parades. New flags bearing the twisted cross, or swastika, flew from many street poles and Gentile homes, and were proudly held high by the enthusiastic paraders as they marched down the streets.

Anti-Jewish voices were becoming louder each day, soon reaching a feverish pitch. Now everyone had to listen to them, to finally take them seriously. Jews watched in horror when their Gentile neighbors gave the Nazi salute, "Heil Hitler!"

In synagogue on the Sabbath, rumors that some Jewish families planned to leave Kippenheim for safer havens were whispered quietly among the congregants. Papa had been hearing the ugly screams and warnings along with everyone else, but he still brushed them off half-heartedly.

"Rina, we live so close to the borders of France and Switzerland. If things get too hot, we can always make a dash for it. We still don't have to worry yet!"

Those words would soon be only philosophical. The turbulent storm was about to strike even the sleepy little village of Kippenheim.

KRISTALLNACHT

My childhood was irreparably disrupted on a cold November morning in 1938. The immense storm clouds that had been threatening Jewish lives finally burst with thundering vengeance. It was two months before my fourth birthday.

Kristallnacht, the "Night of Broken Glass," began on November 9, 1938, in both Germany and Austria. It lasted two horrifying days.

Almost all Jewish houses of worship were severely desecrated, and where possible, burned to the ground. Jewish homes and businesses were looted and destroyed. Shattered glass lay everywhere in the Jewish houses.

Many Jewish men were arrested and sent to concentration camps. Those who resisted were badly beaten or shot to death.

My grandparents had come to visit us in Kippenheim, and were caught along with us in the unforgettable terror. Opa had gone to the synagogue early for the morning prayer. He had no clue that on that day he would be arrested without cause and sent to the Dachau concentration camp in Germany.

Not even the synagogue could offer safety to the worshipers. Men wearing the traditional prayer shawls, deep in prayer, felt safe in the embrace of the cloth draped over their shoulders. They thought that the Almighty's arms surrounded and shielded them from harm. But this time was different. There was no protection.

Papa was rudely awakened by a loud banging on the large front door. It was the police, come to arrest him. He was told to report to the courtyard of the City Hall, where he would join all the other Jewish men of Kippenheim. Not even the teenage boys above the age of 16 were spared.

Some of the sacred Torah scrolls, which were made of parchment, were removed from the sanctuary, torn apart, and draped around the fearful men, in total disrespect for their religion.

Only women and children were left behind in the village. Although the synagogue was set aflame, the fire was quickly extinguished for fear that the neighboring Christian houses might also suffer damage. Nevertheless, the whole inside of the building had been damaged, and the holy sanctuary had been desecrated. The Ten Commandments were dislodged from their perch on top of the structure and thrown to the ground. This served as a warning that from that point on, laws of decency and humanity were dead.

A long night, one which would plunge most of Europe into darkness, was approaching.

I remember standing in the living room with Oma, Frau Ketterer, and Mama, who was holding my hand tightly. Our maid, Liesa, had recently left, feeling that it was too dangerous for her to continue employment in a Jewish home.

We clung to each other as stones flew through our windows, shattering them one by one. Pieces of glass fell all around us, covering the floor with the glittering jagged pieces.

We could hear the sound of breaking glass throughout our large 16 room house. One of the hoodlums peered through a broken window, noticing the still intact chandelier hanging from the ceiling. We heard a blood-curdling cry coming from the street.

"Quick, let's smash this one!" And a brick hit its mark, barely missing me.

Mama pulled me to safety. We fled to a secluded shed in the courtyard of our house. There we stood in complete silence, hardly breathing, cowering in fear. We prayed that the mob would not storm the house and find us.

The thugs kept banging loudly on the large door that gave entrance to our courtyard, which was where Papa parked his large black car. Frau Ketterer quickly disappeared as soon as the commotion began. As soon as the first window was shattered, sending flying glass in all directions, she ran to an exit in the courtyard. where she could not be seen leaving a Jewish house. She feared, probably correctly, that being with Jewish people could bring harm to her family.

This left just Mama and me, clinging to each other in desperation. Our hearts pounded loudly enough to disclose our hiding place. It was the first time in my young life that I felt a fear greater even than the time when, as a two and a half year old, I had fallen and opened my cheek.

At that time, I was in mortal fear about what Papa would say when he came home. Would he punish me, since I had not obeyed Frau Ketterer's pleas to stop running across the carpet in the first floor hallway?

Frau Ketterer had warned me that if I did not listen to her, she would pull the rug from under me when I ran across the carpet. And she did. I of course fell, and the sharp corner of the bannister on the staircase dug into my upper left cheek, barely missing my eye. My mother rushed me to Dr. Weber's office, where he had me sit on my mother's lap while he stitched my wound.

But this time was far worse than my fall and a few stitches. I cringed at the violence around me, not understanding the reason for what was happening.

Finally the rioting stopped, and the silence of the night clothed the earlier fury. We waited, not moving, hoping that the hoodlums were not tricking us, not stealthily waiting to discover us in our hiding place.

More time elapsed, but we could hear no repetition of the screams and loud banging on the door. Mama decided that we should leave the shed, and we took the same route to leave the house that Frau Ketterer had taken a few hours before. Like her, no one would see us leaving the house.

We spent the night with our Jewish neighbors, the Wertheimer family. Their windows had also been broken, and the men of the household arrested.

Eventually all the shattered windows were boarded up to keep out the cold November wind. We were made personally responsible for the damage, and had to pay for the replacement windows.

The entire community was in a state of shock. The hateful words we had been hearing on the radio had come true.

Miraculously, Papa and Opa were released from the Dachau concentration camp a few weeks later. They had both been dreadfully mistreated. Even Papa's war record and Iron Cross had had no affect on the guards. Papa had a rude awakening of how Jews were to be treated in the "New Order."

It was time to leave Germany, but Papa had hesitated too long and the doors to the free world had almost completely shut. Opa had never wanted to leave his beloved Jebenhausen, though. "Here," he said, "is where I was born. Here is where I will die!"

Our lives changed drastically when Papa returned from Dachau. We had finally been awakened from our slumber of complacency.

In 1939, having packed all our belongings, we sold our house for a low price. Our destination was my grandparents' house in Jebenhausen. We still had hopes of leaving Germany, and therefore planned to stay in Jebenhausen for only a short time.

In Jebenhausen, Opa's wish to die in his own home was soon granted. His sick heart had weakened even more during his stay in Dachau. Soon after our arrival, he peacefully entered into eternal sleep, cradled in my parents' arms.

My grandparents' maid, Therese, had been in their employ for 25 years, but since Mama would help out with the chores, Therese was no longer needed after our arrival. Although it was not wise for Therese to continue to work for Jews, she continued her friendship with us, bringing us food when we were no longer permitted to shop in certain stores.

Papa was forced by the Nazi Order to sell his textile business, and Opa sold his last cows. We had to live off our savings, and felt our money rapidly diminishing.

Our standard of living was critically changed, since no new money was coming in. We bought only the necessities needed to sustain our lives.

I had never thought myself any different from my Gentile playmates in Jebenhausen. Although anti-Jewish feelings in Germany had become even more virulent after the massive November riots, the children of Jebenhausen were not yet infected with the disease of hatred. They continued their friendships with me, including me in their games as they had before.

My leadership qualities showed up early in life. Perhaps this was inherited through my father's genes.

It was I who would lead Elisabeth, Doris, Gerlinde, and the other children as we marched up and down the hilly street in Jebenhausen, singing the popular songs, which often contained Nazi propaganda. None of us understood the deeper meaning of the songs. Their infectious rhythms enticed us, and everyone was singing them. Why not us?

Jebenhausen was not spared from the anti-Jewish laws. New restrictive decrees were announced every day. Our hopes of leaving Germany were now only a memory. Jews were compelled to give up all their gold and silver, and as mentioned before, they were not allowed to shop in many of the stores.

Every phase of life was changed for the Jews; they were practically not permitted to breathe. The children had to attend schools especially set up for Jews. The goal was utter degradation.

To humiliate the Jews even more, in late 1941 they were forced to sew the yellow Star of David with the word *"Jude"* on the left side of their clothing, right above the heart, in Hebrew-like script. Not even children were spared from this insult.

I needed special "travel permission" documents to attend the only Jewish school in the province of Wuerttemberg. Jews were no longer allowed to travel or move freely at will, without consent.

I had to walk about two miles from Jebenhausen, where I then took the Goeppingen train to Stuttgart. The train ride took about one hour. As a six year old child, it was dangerous for me to ride alone. The Gentile children around me constantly taunted and heckled me. "You dirty Jew!" they jeered.

Papa told me to sit near the left window and lean against it, in order to unobtrusively cover my yellow badge, even though it was strictly forbidden to hide the so-called "mark of shame."

I remember only one incident of kindness: a Gentile woman left a brown paper bag filled with rolls next to my seat on the train. She must have felt sorry for the little Jewish child traveling by herself.

The stranger was a hero to me, since any association with Jews could result in severe punishment—even in death.

Ironically, all Jewish females were ordered to add "Sara" to their names, and the males "Israel." My parents had tried so hard to avoid giving me a typical Jewish name, but from this point on I was "Inge Sara Auerbacher."

Inge at age three, 1938.

The destruction of our synagogue in Kippenheim, 1938.

THE FINAL SOLUTION

Papa's sisters, Paula and Hilde, and their families, had been able to find refuge in Brazil. Aunt Rosel and her new second husband were living in France. Mama's brother, Karl, and his wife, had reached the United States.

None of the family on the outside was able to help us get visas to leave Germany. All their efforts failed; we had waited too long to judge and act upon the danger.

Our fate was now sealed. Escape was no longer possible.

The "Final Solution," the Nazi plan for the total liquidation of all the Jews in Europe, began in 1941, when the first deportations to the "East" began.

Oma and most of my classmates were deported to Riga in Latvia, in December of 1941. Almost all of them were shot in a nearby forest by the Mobile Killing Forces.

We had been spared from being deported at that time because of Papa's World War I injuries. But we were immediately forced out of my grandparents' house, receiving no monetary compensation. The German State now owned my grandparents' house. We were relocated to one of the "Jewish houses" in the neighboring town of Goeppingen.

Soon after our forced relocation, my school was closed. I had not even completed the first grade.

Great Grandma Malchen suddenly died. She had been living a few hours from us. My parents had to get special permission from the government to travel, in order to attend her funeral. We were the only relatives there to place her to her final rest.

Malchen was the mother of 14 children. During World War I, four sons had served in the German Armed Forces. Two had given their lives for the Fatherland. It was very painful to bury a woman without even one of her children at her gravesite; but some of her children had already been killed in concentration camps, while others had left Germany in time and were settled in safe countries.

Deportations to the "East" became more frequent during the following months. None of us knew that the "East" meant a death sentence. But we had fears and no doubts that the "East" denoted something bad for the Jews.

Our turn came on August 22, 1942, when we received our orders for transport. I was now number "XIII-1-408"—the youngest in our transport of about 1200 people. I was only seven years old. My greatest concern was to take along my doll, Marlene, which I did. Oma had given her to me on my second birthday.

Papa was so angry that he danced on top of our polished dining room table in order to mark it with scratches. Crazed with anger, he repeatedly stomped his shoes down on the shiny surface.

"No one is going to get pleasure from my furniture!" he shouted. Mama kept trying to stop him, but he continued until he saw bruises on the table.

The following day, we were on our way to the "East."

Our destination was the Terezin concentration camp in Czechoslovakia. Terezin had large brick barracks, underground cells and old broken-down houses in very poor condition. It was isolated from the outside world by high walls, deep water-filled trenches, wooden fences and barbed wire. Communication with the outside world was strictly forbidden.

Terezin had been a garrison town, abandoned by the military in the 1880s and then settled by a few thousand civilians. By the end of 1941, Terezin had been emptied and readied by high-ranking Nazi officials, to serve as a transit camp for Jewish deportees. From Terezin the deportees were slated for extermination in the gas chambers of Auschwitz and other death camps located in Poland.

All of our clothing, except for what we wore, was confiscated upon our arrival. We never saw our suitcases again. I arrived in Terezin thankfully holding my doll in my arms, dragging a small duffel bag, a metal dish, and a spoon.

I contracted scarlet fever soon after our arrival in Terezin, and spent four months in the so-called hospital, a room whose peeling walls were covered with flies. Each bed was occupied by two children.

Measles, mumps, and a double middle ear infection followed. I was infested with worms, I lost my voice, and my body was covered with boils. I was not expected to live. But miraculously, just before my eighth birthday I recovered and was permitted to rejoin my parents.

Most men, women, and children were housed in separate quarters. I was lucky to be allowed to stay with my parents in the disabled war veterans section. Life was harsh and strange, without privacy. We slept on the floor or, if fortunate, on straw-filled mattresses, packed like sardines on double and triple-deck bunk beds. The living quarters were unbearably hot in the summer and very cold in the winter.

We stood in line three times a day, our metal dishes in hand, to receive our daily food rations from the community kitchens. Bread, potatoes and soup were the most important words in our vocabulary. Breakfast consisted of coffee, a dark-colored liquid which had a horrible aftertaste. Lunch was a watery soup, a potato, and a small portion of turnips, or a sauce containing slivers of horse meat. Dinner was soup.

Eventually the camp's population swelled to 60,000. From 1941 to 1945, 140,000 people passed through Terezin. Every inch of space was utilized.

There were constant epidemics, due to overcrowding and lack of hygiene. Rats, mice, fleas and bedbugs were a constant menace for us.

I can still feel the awful stomach cramps from dysentery, which hounded everyone, and the long walks to the latrines, which were always crowded and without privacy.

Almost all the adults were forced to work. Mama's first job was washing laundry from typhus patients. Although she had no training in nursing, she later worked as a nurse in the old people's hospital for sick women.

Every day Papa rummaged in the garbage dump in search of potato peelings and rotten turnips to supplement our meager diet. We lived in constant fear that we would be sent further east into the unknown, where conditions could be even worse than those in Terezin.

I belonged to a flock of children who lived within our compound. There was my best friend, Ruth, who shared my bunk bed, and Werner, Rolf, Gerda, and her older sister, Margot. School was absolutely forbidden, but some heroic teachers taught us in so-called "keeping busy classes," mostly from memory since there were very few books or school supplies.

Our bodies became thinner with each passing day, and our bones began to show through our skin. Still, we continued to play, rummaging in the garbage heaps hoping to find a treasure—a rotten turnip, potato peelings, or a piece of string.

Because of the poor nutrition, crowded living conditions and lack of hygiene, Terezin was an ideal breeding ground for many contagious diseases.

It was whispered among our parents that Gerda was sick with a bad illness, which we could catch.

"Don't go near her, please!" Ruth and I were warned. We wondered what this terrible sickness could be.

Gerda sat in the sun in the dirty backyard that separated the houses. She looked sad sitting all alone with no one to play with. I was jealous of her, since she received a small portion of milk powder and some extra food rations. Whatever she had, it was worth it, I thought. I, too, wanted to get more food. I prayed with all my heart to get the same sickness.

One day I overheard my parents speaking about Gerda's mystery sickness. "Gerda has tuberculosis."

What could be so terrible about this disease, I wondered. *Gerda doesn't look too different from us.* I did notice that she tired easily as we played, though; and Ruth's parents also looked very serious when they spoke to her about our friend.

"You must stay away from Gerda," they repeated frequently in pleading tones.

None of us had ever heard the word "tuberculosis" before, but the sound of the word had a foreboding feeling of danger. I knew about scarlet fever and most of the other so-called childhood diseases, but the term "tuberculosis" seemed to belong to another category. I had never known anyone who had been sick with it. Had I not recuperated from all my previous illnesses? Surely I would also become well from this one too, if I caught it, I thought.

Soon afterward, most of the children in the camp were tested for tuberculosis. And somehow my prayers were answered: I tested positive.

Now I, too, will get a special food ration like Gerda.

Ruth, who was even thinner than I, tested negative. This was a puzzle to me. My parents were upset, but testing positive did not necessarily mean that my case was active. It meant that I had been exposed to the bug causing tuberculosis and that my body was reacting to it.

But before long, I started to get the same symptoms as Gerda. I felt very tired at times, just like her, and I started coughing. My parents fervently hoped that my condition would not worsen.

Gerda was eventually hospitalized, a situation which put her in grave danger of being sent to the "East." Luckily my own symptoms did not become that severe, and I therefore did not share the same possible fate.

Transports came to Terezin and then went to unknown destinations. They reached a crescendo during the Jewish High Holidays in 1944. When the last selections to the "East" were made, all remaining disabled war veterans had to appear at SS

Headquarters. A red circle was drawn around my family's names. We had been spared from certain death.

My friends, Ruth, Werner, Rolf, and their parents, did not fare as well. They were herded into the waiting cattle cars. The doors were bolted, their fates were sealed, and within a few days of their departure, their lives were snuffed out in the gas chambers of Auschwitz.

****

The war was finally coming to an end. On May 8, 1945, my parents and I were finally liberated by the Soviet Army, which was a member of the Allied Forces. Miraculously, Gerda also made it out of this hell. Only a few thousand survivors were left alive in Terezin to be rescued. Out of the 15,000 children sent to Terezin, very few survived.

The inmates of Terezin had come from many countries in Europe, from all walks of life and from different professions. Some were even people of mixed Jewish and Christian origin. Being only part Jewish was a sufficient credential to earn you a position in a concentration camp.

But now the nightmare that had befallen the Jews and the world was finally over. Life, such as it was for the newly emancipated survivors, who suffered both physical and spiritual damage, was about to begin.

THE AFTERMATH

In early July, 1945, we were finally picked up by a bus from the city of Stuttgart, Germany. It felt as if a carriage had descended from heaven to take us away from the man-created hell of Terezin. There were 13 survivors from our original transport of about 1200 people. Among them were my parents and I. It was a miracle that a complete family unit had managed to survive the Nazi death machine.

After a short stay in a displaced persons' camp in Stuttgart, a temporary facility which had been prepared to house returning Jewish refugees, we made our way back to Jebenhausen, where we hoped to be reunited with my grandmother.

It became apparent that many members of our family would never return home, including my beloved Oma. Grandma had become a victim of the mobile killing squads in a forest near Riga in Latvia. The others had all lost their lives to the Nazis by starvation, gassing or firing squads. None of the Jewish victims would ever be granted a proper burial or a permanent resting place. Only ashes, mass graves with a token covering of earth, and anonymity, remained.

Events moved at a quick pace, and life returned to almost normal.

We soon had a nicely furnished apartment in Goeppingen, a larger town than Jebenhausen. Papa owned a car once again, a Mercedes, and he resumed his wholesale textile business.

Very few other Jewish children had survived the years of torture in the state of Wuerttemberg or elsewhere throughout Europe. I had lost almost four years of school, and was placed in fourth and fifth grade classes.

It was hard to believe that one could have a reasonably normal life after such horror and misery. I was ten years old, and felt that I had already lived a lifetime of experiences. And now I was thrust into a new life and a new role, that of being a child once again. It all felt very strange and unsettling.

Jewish-American soldiers often came to our home and showered me with candy and sometimes with ice cream. Two of them in particular stand out in my memory: Danny Smolens and Sid Bernstein, both of whom hailed from Boston. I felt very special, and sometimes shared my goodies with my new Christian friends. Food was very scarce in postwar Germany, and all goods were hard to come by. Everything had become a luxury.

Despite our "good" (relatively speaking) life, my parents decided to leave Germany less than a year after our return. They thought that there was no future for me in the blood-drenched land of my birth, even though it was said there was a "new wind" blowing in Germany.

In 1946, President Harry S. Truman, as a gesture of good will, opened the doors of America for the Jewish survivors of Hitler's hell. My parents wanted to take advantage of this offer, and applied to be included on the first list.

We had to go through a medical examination. No x-rays were taken, thank goodness. I felt well again and my parents did not volunteer the information that I had tested positive for tuberculosis in the past. We knew that anyone with a contagious disease would not be able to get clearance, especially a person afflicted with tuberculosis. I had gained weight, felt fine, and all of us assumed that I was free of disease.

To our surprise we were selected to be on the first boat. Papa had to decline the offer since he had to dispose of his business first and had not had time to do so. But we were ready for the second boat, and left shortly afterward.

It was now the spring of 1946. Since very few passenger trains were available after the war, cattle cars were used to transport us to the port of Bremerhaven. None of us minded sleeping on the floor; we were used to such conditions.

The nights were cool, and it was chilly in the box car. There were a few cots, but not enough for everyone. Since I was the youngest in our car, I was given a bed.

The passage on the American troop transport ship, the Marine Perch, took ten days. It was a very stormy crossing, but we finally arrived in the New York City harbor on May 24, 1946.

We soon found ourselves in Rockville Center, a suburb of New York City, together with Mama's brother Karl, his wife Trudl, and Trudl's father. Uncle Karl had fought as an American soldier in some of the bloodiest battles of World War II, and had returned home only recently.

With our arrival, it became very crowded in Uncle Karl's small apartment. We knew that the situation could be only temporary, so while my parents searched for work, I was placed for a few weeks with distant relatives in Jamaica, in the borough of Queens. They had a daughter close to my age and an older son.

Within a short time, more permanent living quarters were found. My parents accepted jobs as domestics for a wealthy Jewish family in Rye, New York. We were given two rooms and a bathroom for our exclusive use.

Mama and Papa worked very hard for little pay and almost no time off. They were not happy with their situation, but did not dare complain, since we needed a roof over our heads. Their main concern was not to be a burden to anyone and not to "cause waves."

I fared much better than my parents. The three children of the house permitted me to join them in their play. It was great fun running around the large estate grounds, and I was content and happy.

These "normal" times were suddenly interrupted. I began to tire easily. Running around with the children became an effort. I preferred to rest and take frequent naps.

It was as if some elusive force had sucked all the energy out of me. Mama thought that this was caused by a cold that I had been harboring for some time. She blamed its origin on the chilly box car. My cough, which had been minor up to this point, now became increasingly more severe.

Mama was deeply concerned. Mrs. Nadler, her employer, also noticed the change in me, and she began to worry that her children might catch my awful cold. She recommended that I see her family physician. An appointment was made, and Mrs. Nadler drove Mama and me to the office.

The doctor examined me thoroughly, but was not satisfied with his findings. In a stern voice he suggested that I see Dr. Childress, the Chief of Chest Diseases at Grasslands Hospital in Valhalla, New York.

Our worst fears came true after Dr. Childress examined me. "Your daughter," he said, "has pulmonary tuberculosis!"

The words cut like a knife into our hearts. I hardly heard his last words: "And she must be hospitalized as soon as possible!" All I remember hearing was the word "hospital."

"No, no, I'm not going to a hospital," I sobbed, tears streaming down my face. I didn't want to be separated from my parents again, and I certainly knew what a hospital was like from my past experience with scarlet fever at Terezin.

Now it became clear in my mind: *Didn't I pray for this disease, so that I would receive a greater ration of food?* But then I had felt well again, and I thought that the disease would disappear forever as soon as we were set free. It belonged to the concentration camp time, I thought, not to my present life. People in America don't get sick with tuberculosis, people have enough food to eat. I saw the mountains of chocolate and other items in the store windows. No one seemed to go hungry here.

Why me, why me, God, at this time—just as things are going so well for me! God, I don't want this sickness now. You answered my prayers in the past, did you forget that I don't need to be sick anymore? I'm very angry with you. I don't want to be sick and have to go to a hospital!

I was admitted to Sunshine Cottage, the children's communicable disease hospital at Grasslands, in July, 1946. *Didn't God listen to my prayers anymore? Have I misbehaved so badly that I have to be punished with this unexpected sentence?*

I soon found myself in Ward 200, the tuberculosis section of the hospital. There was another ward downstairs which served children afflicted with polio.

There was still a great stigma associated with tuberculosis. It was considered a curse. People were afraid to be near such patients because of the infectious nature of the disease. It was best not to advertise it; this was not considered to be like any other sickness, this was associated with shame.

Mrs. Nadler, shocked to hear the news about my illness, soon dismissed my parents. She feared that if my parents were permitted to stay, her family would have a chance to be infected with my disease.

This is only a nightmare, I thought. *I will surely wake up soon, and find myself in good health again.* But to my disappointment the situation was real.

I was surrounded by many boys and girls, most of them on complete bed rest, the popular treatment plan at the time. There were no magic drugs that could cure tuberculosis; either you responded to bed rest, or you might face more drastic treatments like surgery or pneumothorax. Pneumothorax meant having air pumped into the pleural cavity to collapse the sick lung, to give it complete rest for a period of time. The outlook for improvement in health was not very promising. Many people did not respond and were ultimately consumed by the disease.

Since pneumothorax was frequently unsuccessful, my parents thankfully didn't permit it to be performed on me. Tuberculosis is a chronic disease; at the time the best one could hope for was to arrest and encapsulate the deadly bacillus with a calcium shell. But even if the TB was arrested, there was always great danger that the calcifications might rupture and start the active disease process once again.

I immediately had to undergo many painful tests. All of us had to endure a "gastric" test every other week, sometimes more often. We knew that it was our turn when we weren't served breakfast.

The doctors performing the procedure were usually inexperienced interns. They came armed with kidney-shaped metal pans in which long rubber hoses sat like snakes ready to attack. Some of the tubes appeared thicker than others. The procedure entailed inserting and guiding one of the long rubber hoses through the nose and down toward the stomach.

We all pleaded, "Please, doctor, give me the thinnest one so that it won't hurt so much."

The doctors always answered, "They are all the same size. Don't make a fuss! Let's get it over with, I have to do many today."

We were given a piece of ice to suck on when gagging overwhelmed us. Most of the time I pushed the tube down by myself, thus regulating the pain.

"More, more, push it down more," the young doctor commanded without any emotion in his voice.

When the desired depth was reached, a syringe was attached to the tube and a clear liquid was withdrawn. This sample was sent to the laboratory for analysis. A positive result of the culture meant that the disease was still active and not under control.

There was an even greater torture which we all feared: the bronchoscopy. This procedure was performed in the operating room. I had to endure this test only one time, but the memory of the terrible pain is still strong in my mind. Very little anesthesia was given. I was told to gargle with a bad tasting solution, which lightly iced my throat for a little while, but not for the duration of the procedure. A long instrument was snaked deep into my bronchial tubes. The pain was excruciating. You couldn't even scream, because the instrument was touching the vocal chords.

In my mind, the test took a very long time. I thought that I would choke to death. When the instrument was finally removed, I was surprised to find that I was still alive. I begged my parents not to sign for such a test again, even though it was recommended by the doctors. They granted my wish, and I never had to endure that particular torture again.

Periodically we were sent to a conference, where attending physicians and resident doctors in training were assembled. When my turn came, I overheard Dr. Childress say as he discussed my case, "Here is a child who was in one of the Nazi camps. She has a bad case—both of the lungs are involved."

I was considered one of the sickest children in Ward 200. I was not permitted to leave my bed for more than a year, and then it was only for a short period each time. I was in a place which seemed like another prison to me. I had been liberated from the Terezin concentration camp for less than two years, and much of this time had been spent in the hospital. *Would I ever be able to enjoy freedom again?*

We had improvised schooling when we were up to it. Our teacher, Miss Kohn, came to our bedsides and brought us texts and workbooks, though there were times when my lessons were stopped because of the worsening of my illness.

Sunshine Cottage could not be compared to the hospital in Terezin. The hospital was staffed mainly by student nurses and aids, the majority of whom were very kind to us. But although it was not a prison, it nevertheless took away my freedom.

I worked hard to learn English, and I soon began to think in English instead of in German. My parents brought me a radio and I listened to it often, which helped me gain better language skills.

I longed to see my parents more often. They were permitted to visit me only for a couple of hours once a week, on Sundays. It was the best day of the week for me.

My best friend was still my doll, Marlene, who had been my constant companion since I was two years old. She sat on a metal dresser next to my bed.

I shared my room with three black girls, with whom I became friends. Ward 200 was divided into a "Girls" end and a "Boys" end, both of which contained children of all different racial and ethnic backgrounds.

I was the only Jewish child in the entire hospital. Once again I felt isolated, not only because I was in a hospital, but also because there was no one with whom I could have a religious bond. Everyone else celebrated the Christian holidays, and I even had to eat food forbidden in the Jewish faith, since no special provisions were made for me to honor Jewish dietary laws.

At times, not wanting to be different, I joined my new friends in celebrating Christian holidays. But my conscience often got the better of me. I felt guilty eating pork and having a small Christmas tree near my bed, which had been given to me as a special gesture of friendship.

It was still strange for me to see so many black people in America. I had never seen a black person before my liberation from the concentration camp. A black-American soldier had come to Terezin, and some of the few surviving children had run to look at him. I was afraid to shake hands with him, but a brave girl did it quickly, hoping that his color would not come off on her when she pulled her hand away.

We all looked to see if the dark brown color had rubbed off on her. There was no change, of course; her hand appeared to be the same. We were bewildered. The soldier, who was friendly and wanted to be kind to us, gave us candy and laughed at our surprise.

I realized during my hospitalization that despite differences in color and religion, we were all just a group of children with the same dream of getting well and being able to leave Ward 200.

A sad fact, incidentally, was that a few of the children's parents had also contracted tuberculosis, and were hospitalized in the adult section of the medical center. There were times when a mother or father died of the disease, leaving their child bereft and lonely.

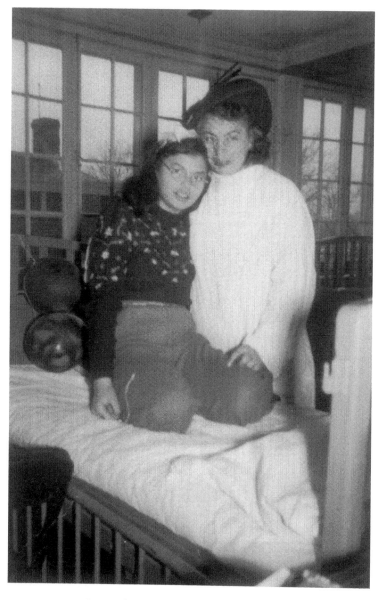

Inge and Mama at Sunshine Cottage, 1947.

CHANGING
TIMES

I was 13 years old in 1948. Two years had passed and I was still in the hospital, on complete bed rest almost the entire time.

My parents finally convinced the doctors to allow me to go home to Brooklyn, where they had rented a cold water flat on the third floor of a walk-up on Chauncey Street in the neighborhood of Bushwick. The doctors granted their wish with great trepidation, since my health had not improved much. They imposed specific regulations: Dishes must be kept separate, since I was still contagious; I had to rest a few hours a day; I was not to participate in any strenuous activities.

At home with my loving parents, I finally began to get stronger each day. But I had no friends, and since I was not allowed to go to public school, I felt very lonely. Sometimes I almost wished I were back in the hospital. At least there I had many companions.

Eventually I was no longer contagious, but still not well enough to enter a normal life.

It took some time before Papa was able to find a friend for me. Papa had met Louise's father during a synagogue service. They lived only one block away, but unfortunately I didn't get to see her often, since she was busy with school and with other friends. I didn't reveal the nature of my sickness to her, lest I lose her friendship.

Papa by now had his own peddling business. He sold dry goods on credit, mainly to German immigrants who lived in Ridgewood, Brooklyn, and in some nearby cities in New Jersey.

Mama and I decided that we could help out financially by selling aprons to people in the neighborhood. We knocked on many apartment doors. The "two ladies with the nice aprons" became part of the Chauncey Street scene. Women paid installments of 50 cents each week in order to buy our aprons. I walked up and down the high stairs, never telling my mother when I got tired. I was too excited and happy with our success to complain.

Just as everything was falling into place, my cough returned, much more severely than before. Once again I became very weak and felt tired all the time. Maybe climbing all those stairs during our selling trips had been harmful to me.

Mama felt guilty for having allowed me to join her in our new endeavor, and ordered me to stay at home and rest. I felt sad and disappointed, not only because I was sick, but because I couldn't help her.

One day while I was in the bathroom I coughed especially hard and tasted something salty in my mouth. I took a tissue and wiped my mouth, seeing with horror that the white color of the tissue was marred with a brilliant large red spot. Blood!

I quickly swallowed the rest of the fluid in my mouth, fearing that my mother might notice it. I made sure that the tissue was discarded by flushing it down the toilet. But after repeated attempts to swallow the blood, it started to come through my nose. I tried hard to conceal the blood from my parents, but as time went on, the hemorrhaging became stronger and more frequent, and I could no longer hide my horrific secret.

My parents and I were devastated. I thought, *Is this the way you feel when you're dying?*

I didn't have enough strength to walk, and my father had to carry me to the car for my appointment with the doctor, who was located in Scarsdale. The doctor, who had taken care of me in the hospital, examined me carefully. Since my health had worsened and long rides would now be too taxing for me, he advised my parents to find a specialist nearer to our home.

My parents feared the worst. "Did we survive the concentration camp only to suffer again? Our Inge must overcome this cursed sickness!"

The new doctor immediately put me on a new experimental drug—streptomycin. I recalled that a boy in the hospital had been put on the same medication. He had a different type of tuberculosis, with open wounds under his arms. The streptomycin worked like a miracle. He got well after a few months, and went home.

The drug, however, had a serious possible side effect: in some cases it caused deafness. None of the children with tuberculosis of the lungs or bones had yet been treated with it.

Mama was taught how to inject me with the drug twice a day. She felt more emotional pain giving these needles to me than I did getting them, so a nurse was found to continue my injections, which had to be given intra-muscularly into my buttocks.

The needles burned and hurt, and when my behind became too sore, my legs and arms were also used for the injections.

The new drug worked miracles. My condition improved quickly, and I became stronger each day. I no longer coughed, and the hemorrhaging stopped. Even better, the possible side effect of hearing loss didn't occur.

The doctor was ecstatic. He explained to my parents that streptomycin was fairly new, and still experimental. But since I was so critically ill, he had decided to take a chance with it.

Streptomycin was the first drug ever to find success in the treatment of tuberculosis. My parents were overjoyed that the medicine was finally available, clearly just in time to save my life. The old treatment of bed rest had failed me through the years. And although it took many months to bring full recovery, I was now on my way back to good health.

I felt very lucky, and thought of the children still in the hospital. Had they been given this new drug? Had any of them gotten to go home?

My questions would never be answered, since I had severed all ties when I left the hospital. I had wanted to leave the past behind and start a new life, but nevertheless I found that I was curious about my old friends.

Finally, at age 15, I was able to enter Bushwick High School in Brooklyn, where I began my real school career for the first time. I wanted to become the best student in the school, so I worked hard in all my studies. Sometimes, though, I felt painfully lost, since I had missed so many formal years of schooling.

To my dismay, I was the oldest student in the class. Most students entered high school at the age of 14 or even younger. The age difference bothered me greatly, and to remedy the situation I attended summer school three times. Because of my summer school sessions, I was able to complete high school in three years. Best of all, no one had ever learned about my secret past.

My parents were very proud when I received honors in various subjects at my graduation in June, 1953. My best subject was science, and I planned to enter Queens College of the City University of New York as a pre-medical student, with hopes of becoming a physician. I wanted to pursue a career that combined science with social service. After all, I had been surrounded most of my life by doctors, and this seemed to be a logical choice.

My parents bought a house in Jamaica, Queens, in the spring of 1953. I would be the first in my family to go to college.

A NEW LIFE

The summer of 1953 was very special for me. I was 18 years old. I was on fire, wanting to make up for all my lost time in a few steamy weeks before entering college. My health status was excellent; I felt as if I had never before had any serious problems. Even in retrospect, I can hardly think of a time when life was better than those magical weeks.

When I looked in the mirror the image smiling back at me was of a rather attractive teenager. I had slimmed down and was proud of my new looks.

As a child and young teenager, I had always been encouraged to eat large portions of food. "This will help you get better sooner," Mama always said. The result had been a very overweight young girl. But now things were different!

My parents were surprised at how quickly I changed from a shy young girl, a personality trait I had acquired during my years of isolation, to a spunky teenager. I was once again the take-charge person of my early childhood years. I joined a Jewish youth group, where I was popular with the boys, and I dated almost every night, going to movies, seeing plays, and dancing the nights away.

Even my strict parents didn't interfere with my new-found adventures. I could hardly believe my good fortune: I was just like any other teenage girl. The painful injections had been worth it; the miracle fluid forced into my body had given me life. It was like being reborn. I had cheated death once again.

By the end of the summer I had lost more weight, and I looked almost too thin. I never wanted the summer to end, and I became apprehensive when it was time to begin my college career.

Would I do well? Could I compete with my fellow students? Everyone at Queens College entered with a high grade average. The competition was keen, I would no longer have the "star" status that I had worked for and enjoyed at Bushwick. All the other students entering Queens also had top ranking in their high school classes.

The college application didn't seem threatening at first. I answered the first few questions easily. And then my heart almost stopped.

"Have you ever been hospitalized? Explain in detail."

How should I handle this? If I revealed my story, they might order further tests and not accept me. I could not leave the space blank, and decided to answer "Yes" in an illegible scrawl. But I didn't give more details, and hoped they would ignore my scribble.

To my surprise, there was an additional problem. All new students were required to have a chest x-ray. I was nervous, as I didn't want anyone to know about my past. I knew that the calcified scars from the arrested tuberculosis would always remain in my lungs, and would show up on the x-ray.

After only a few weeks at Queens, my worst nightmare came true. The medical office at the college found my x-rays suspicious, and requested that I see a private doctor for further testing. I was afraid, since there were signs of impending doom: once again I felt unusually tired a good part of the day, and I had lost a great deal of weight.

The torture of the gastric test faced me again. My pleading words to the doctor not to give it to me fell on deaf ears. I had thought for sure that streptomycin—the miracle drug—had cured me forever. But to my dismay, the murderous bacillus was on the warpath again.

My doctor's verdict was straight and to the point. "I have bad news. You are sick again!"

I was in a state of shock. I could barely wait to be alone in my room, when all my pent up anger poured out of me. A river of tears soaked my pillow. I hoped my parents would not hear my sobbing. *Would this sickness curse me forever?*

My college career was over after only six short weeks. I was back on complete bed rest. Large doses of streptomycin were ordered.

My parents befriended a woman physician who had a practice in the neighborhood. She came twice a day to inject me with the life-saving viscous fluid.

By this time, two new drugs had been discovered for the treatment of tuberculosis—PAS and INH. The bacillus in me was so virulent that it had become resistant to any single drug. To ensure my recovery, the medical protocol was to use all three drugs. The chemotherapy consisted of a combination of 26 pills a day. My arms, legs and buttocks were sore from injections, and the pills made me nauseous most of the time. I could hardly eat anything, I was deeply depressed and didn't want to fight the deadly bug anymore. I wanted to die!

I could not understand why I should be subjected to more torture, once again having to be forced to live like an outcast. Would a microscopic bacillus determine my life and dreams forever, an enemy so small yet so powerful that it could consume and suck all life out of me? Must I be at its mercy forever?

****

To help us pay our mortgage, my parents rented out single rooms on the second floor of our new home. It soon became too difficult for my mother constantly to walk up to our bedrooms in the third floor converted attic to tend to me, so I was placed on a couch which we moved into the living room on the first floor. This made it easier for my mother to take care of me, and there was a television there to entertain me and to help keep my mind off my terrible situation.

One day a young man from the next door rang our bell. He inquired about renting a room for his friend. Seeing me in bed, he began to speak with me.

Murray was in his late twenties, and Jewish. He had curly dark-brown hair, was rather handsome, and he possessed a wonderfully lively personality. He had studied psychology in college.

Murray and I became close friends. He visited me almost every weekend, and I looked forward to our intellectual discussions. He often surprised me with a book or with one of his favorite records to play on my new record player. I enjoyed listening to the music.

We soon fell in love.

One day he questioned me about the large glass jar filled with pills next to my bed. I was afraid to tell him the truth, and said they were vitamins. I was happy that he didn't pester me to find out more about my sickness. I certainly was not going to volunteer any information. However, I avoided his advances to kiss me, in order to protect him from becoming infected with TB. I made all kinds of excuses, which he seemed to accept.

Murray brought joy to my life again. And soon I was no longer feeling constantly nauseous. Streptomycin once again had helped me to survive. It was like a general leading an army on the battlefield to victory and to life.

My relationship with Murray came to an abrupt end after a few months. He told me that he had not been honest with me, that he was married. He had rented the room next door when he had separated from his wife, but now they had reconciled and were going to resume their marriage.

I was devastated. I felt cheated. I reminded myself, though, that I also had not been honest with him. I never did get around to telling him the nature of my illness.

After a year, I returned to Queens College. Once again I was behind in my classes. I continued my studies with the hope of attaining a Bachelor of Science degree in chemistry, with plans to eventually work in medical research. My dreams of becoming a physician had ended; the strain of the profession would have been too much for me.

My girlfriend Louise was two years ahead of me at Queens, majoring in English. New Year's Eve was always a desperate time for both of us. Too soon we entered December, 1955, and neither of us had dates for the magical evening a bare four weeks away. I decided that we should go to a dance, where we would hopefully meet someone.

Louise was not anxious to join me at the Jewish Singles Club in Manhattan. She had a Latin test coming up, and being an over-achieving student, didn't want to risk losing her high rank in class by doing poorly. I was determined to go, however, and went to the dance alone.

I was soon approached by an attractive dark blond-haired young man. He was just tall enough to suit my qualifications. Henry spoke with a heavy Slavic accent. To my joy, he also liked science, and was working as a veterinarian at a large animal hospital and adoption center.

Henry and his family had come from Poland, having safely hidden in the vast wilderness of Siberia during World War II. He showed his serious intentions soon after our first meeting, with nightly phone calls and frequent dates. He even introduced me to his family.

New Year's Eve was approaching. December 31 also marked my 21st birthday. I had a feeling that Henry would propose to me on this special night. I had a talk with my mother about how I should handle the story of my health history.

Mama's advice was honest and to the point. "When two people love each other, they must accept each other's good and bad points. Remember the marriage vow, 'In sickness and in health.' Only God is perfect."

And Mama most definitely spoke from personal experience. Papa was not perfect. He had a severe war injury and was not able to raise his right arm. There were prominent deep-healed scars in his right shoulder. But she accepted this because she loved him.

I had my answer. I would test Henry's love for me.

Henry took me to a Russian nightclub. Just before midnight, he proposed to me. I felt that I could not accept his offer before I shared my story with him. I thought that, since he had studied medicine and loved animals, he certainly would not mind my former problem. Anyway, I was once again in excellent health.

After I spoke, Henry looked at me with blank eyes. I felt as if all the lights in the room had suddenly gone out and I was being sucked into a dark abyss.

I was not surprised when Henry cancelled an ice-skating date the following day. I pleaded with him to speak with my doctor. Reluctantly, he agreed to a meeting, but he had apparently already made up his mind. It was over. Once again I cried inside, *Would the curse of TB follow me for the rest of my life?*

I graduated from Queens College with a B.S. degree in Chemistry in June, 1958. Many years of medical research and clinical work followed.

I met a Jewish doctor from Iraq specializing in Physical Medicine, a field stressing physical therapy and rehabilitation. A proposal of marriage came after a short courtship, but once again rejection followed my confession of the history of my health.

I was not sorry for having been honest with a potential marriage partner, but I was deeply saddened that the stigma associated with tuberculosis and the fear that people had would probably follow me forever.

COMING FULL CIRCLE

The years went by and the past became more distant. One day I was watching a television program about a woman survivor who had returned to the places of her torture during her youth. I, too, felt a compulsion to revisit the places of my past. Had all of this been a dream? I had a deep need to confirm everything through adult eyes.

I returned to Sunshine Cottage in 1966. The building was now being used as a teaching facility. I then continued my journey to Germany and to the Terezin Concentration Camp. When I stood in the crematory in Terezin, I was overcome with a sense of responsibility to make the most of my life, to perhaps make up a microcosm of what had been taken from the world.

After my return to America, I decided to apply to medical school. But there were some issues that needed to be considered. I was 31 years old, at that time too old for admission to an American school. I also didn't want to be rejected because of my history of health.

Schools in Europe were more liberal with older students. I decided to apply to a German-speaking country, and selected Heidelberg University in Germany.

My parents and friends were outraged. How could I return to that blood-drenched land! But I felt in my heart that they owed me something, since they had destroyed so much of my life.

To my great surprise, I was accepted when I applied for admission. I left my job as a chemist in a hospital clinical laboratory in the spring of 1968, despite the fact that my boss pleaded with me not to go.

To my great dismay, my parents and friends had been right. Old memories were dying slowly for both sides, and I experienced some unfortunate incidents. I therefore handed in my resignation at the medical school shortly after my enrollment. My dream of becoming a physician was over.

After returning to America, I continued my work as a chemist in a hospital laboratory until my retirement in 1997. I am proud that I worked for 38 years in jobs to preserve life, not in ways to destroy it.

The Nazis took my childhood away through starvation and humiliation, the former of which led to the assault by a deadly microscopic organism and a deeply diseased body. But I had the great fortune of good timing when I was in the most critical stages of tuberculosis: streptomycin was discovered in time to snatch me from the clutches of death.

I found a fulfilling and productive life in science, and I continue to be fulfilled in my writing career and in my work promoting tolerance, acceptance and respect for all people. I am fortunate to have been spared death twice: the first time in the concentration camp, and the second time by streptomycin.

Thank you, Dr. Schatz.

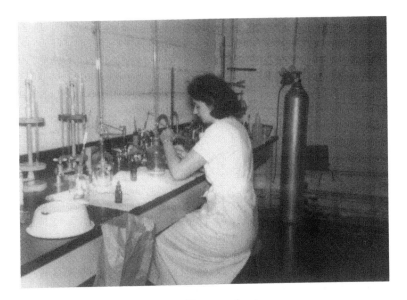

Inge working as a chemist.

FINAL WORDS

Over the years, people have thanked Albert for saving their lives or the lives of their loved ones. He was especially touched by Inge Auerbacher's letter. She has been part of our lives ever since she contacted us.

I am happy that Inge was able to finish Albert's story when he was in bad health during the last years of his life. Our happy life together, along with ultimate world-wide recognition of Albert's achievements, led him to say, the day before he died, "I am at peace with my going."

Vivian Schatz (wife of Albert Schatz)

It is my hope that future young scientists will be recognized for their contributions. There are many stories like this one that have been kept silent for too many years.

May the future be a promising one, with many new discoveries which will someday make all diseases a relic of the past.

It is my heartfelt wish and prayer that all mankind live together in peace, without prejudice, hunger, fear, or torture.

Inge Auerbacher

TRIBUTES TO ALBERT SCHATZ

<u>Doris Jones Ralston, fellow graduate student when Schatz was doing his work at Rutgers University:</u>

Farewell my good friend, Al Schatz. Without you there is a big emptiness around my heart. Knowing you, working with you, laughing with you, and suffering with you has been an important part of my life. Little did I know when I handed you a petri dish culture through the basement window of the Poultry Building that you would discover streptomycin, and that wonderful cures would come, followed by the Nobel Prize for Waksman. You should have been given the chance to share that, and for that I have long ached for you. When he (Waksman) gave his Nobel speech and didn't even mention your name, he proved himself to be a greedy and uncaring person, and I could no longer respect him.

Thank heavens you had a wonderful sense of humor and could go on with a rich and full life. May your spirit soar on forever. It has been a great pleasure knowing you!

Ross M. Tucker, MD, Mayo Clinic, Rochester, Minnesota:

I have been a consultant in Internal Medicine and Nephrology at the Mayo Clinic in Rochester Minnesota since 1964. As such, I had known something about the miraculous discovery of streptomycin in the 1940s. This was the first drug to successfully treat the world wide scourge, tuberculosis. A Mayo Clinic pulmonologist, Corwin Hinshaw, and a veterinarian colleague, William Feldman, had been the first to receive a supply of this precious drug for the experimental treatment of guinea pigs infected with the lethal human form of the Mycobacterium tuberculosis germ. The animals which were treated with streptomycin survived while the untreated control animals perished. I learned subsequently that Albert Schatz, literally working day and night, had prepared these supplies of rather crude streptomycin in his basement laboratories at Rutgers University in New Jersey.

On further inquiry in the year 2000, I located Dr. Schatz in Philadelphia and spent many hours on the phone talking to this dedicated and talented man about his key role in the discovery of the microorganism that produced streptomycin, Streptomyces griseus.

I was saddened to learn that, as the listed co-discoverer of streptomycin on the United States patent, Albert Schatz's name was never mentioned to the visiting Nobel Prize committee members by his Rutgers University department chairman, Selman Waksman. Dr. Waksman subsequently was named as the sole recipient of the 1952 Nobel Prize for Physiology or Medicine, for his role devising techniques that made the discovery of streptomycin possible.

Several months before the actual award was given, a number of members of the scientific community wrote to complain about this grievous oversight. The Nobel Committee members refused to change their mind about excluding the co-discoverer of streptomycin, Albert Schatz.

Another sad aspect of the 1952 Nobel Prize for Physiology or Medicine was the failure to include Corwin Hinshaw in the award. I have in writing that when his former division chairman at Mayo, Dr. Herman Moersch, was interviewed by the visiting Nobel Committee member, Dr. Moersch stated that Dr. Hinshaw did not do enough important work on the drug to warrant his inclusion in the prize that year, even though he (Dr. Hinshaw) and Dr. Feldman had exposed themselves to tubercular animals to prove that infected guinea pigs would survive when given streptomycin. In addition, Hinshaw treated the first human tuberculosis victims in the world with streptomycin at Mayo, and became world renowned for this contribution to medical science. In 1946, Dr. Feldman himself subsequently developed pulmonary tuberculosis and was admitted for treatment in a sanatorium in New Mexico for one year. His treatment included, as you might guess, streptomycin.

All that said, I feel particularly sorry for Albert Schatz, because of the shabby way he was treated by his former mentor and admitted co-discoverer of streptomycin, and by the Nobel Committee who failed to correct a known oversight in the awarding of the 1952 prize for Physiology or Medicine, when they could have done so.

In my mind, Albert Schatz will always be a tragic hero and a wonderful though not generally appreciated man. I hope he will someday receive his just recognition, even though given posthumously.

Dr. Milton Wainwright, Department of Molecular Biology and Biotechnology, University of Sheffield, England:

I first met Albert Schatz in Philadelphia's 30th Street Station. I had arranged to spend a few days with him to discuss his role in the discovery of streptomycin. Streptomycin must have initially generated considerable amounts of money in royalties, so I expected to find Albert and his wife, Vivian, living in the lap of luxury. I was surprised therefore to find that their lifestyle was quite modest, since they were forced to use what monies they received from streptomycin as a regular income, rather than as a source of an opulent life style.

I had been trying to find Albert's whereabouts for the best part of a year and was relieved to be at last interviewing him. In the late 1980s, before the arrival of the internet, I had checked the scientific literature in the hope of finding an academic address for Albert, but to my surprise, there were two references to A. Schatz, one was writing on microbiology and streptomycin, and the other on dentistry. This was a source of confusion until I realized that they were both one and the same person.

I spent an incredibly productive few days with Albert, and learned from him the details of how he discovered streptomycin as a mature graduate student; how he had to fight for a share of the royalties and how he was not even mentioned in the Nobel Prize citation, let alone given a share of the award.

To have been denied a rightful share of a Nobel Prize is of course the biggest professional disappointment any scientist can suffer. All of this was remarkable, because Schatz was senior author on the papers announcing streptomycin to the world; similarly, his name was on the streptomycin patents and was even legally defined as the antibiotics co-discoverer of streptomycin.

By demanding his rights on streptomycin, Albert was called a trouble maker and was shunned by academics in the United States, and initially at least, he found it impossible to make an academic career in the U.S. Many a lesser man would have been destroyed by such treatment. Albert Schatz, however, endured, and with his own strong will and Vivian's ever-present backing, he overcame these obstacles and continued to make a contribution to science throughout his life.

When I interviewed Albert, I was immediately struck by his humanity. He was not the boring, unfeeling scientist of parody. Instead he was a complex, warm person, who was interested in the welfare of others as well as in the environment. Albert had been born into the working class, an origin we both shared, and I well remember his emotional stories of how he saw people go hungry and be mistreated during the Great Depression of the 1930s.

Albert's scientific knowledge was amazing, and he was always a delight to talk to. He was interested in a wide variety of subjects, including some like divining and therapeutic touch which are regarded by some as being fringe science. Such labels did not worry Albert; instead, he was keen to search out enlightenment wherever it could be found. He once told me that all he wanted to do was gain a faculty position somewhere and study the microbes that inhabit the soil. After discovering one of the world's most important life saving drugs, one would have imagined that fate would have allowed him this modest dream. Unfortunately, however, the failings and intrigues of lesser men made this impossible.

It was a privilege to have known Albert Schatz. On his death we lost a modest, humorous and very human man. Albert was an original thinker who, if he had been treated better by American academia, could have made other, maybe even more important, contributions to science and human welfare.

George Alonso, MD, Director of Infection Control and Tuberculosis Services at City Hospital Center at Elmhurst, New York, and Assistant Professor of Medicine at the Mount Sinai School of Medicine:

I had the pleasure of meeting the late Dr. Albert Schatz in September, 2002, when he addressed our medical staff regarding his research on a substance that changed the course of a prehistoric disease that was prevalent throughout the world. Until the discovery of this important drug, efficacious treatments of many deadly infections were beyond the reach of the medical arts. A landmark paper, featuring Dr. Schatz as first author, was published in the *Proceedings of the Society for Experimental Biology and Medicine* in 1944. It described a substance, streptomycin, that affected a broader spectrum of microbial pathogens than was possible with medications available at the time. Among these potentially treatable bacteria was the agent of tuberculosis, one of the plagues of civilization.

Over time, other diseases would also attain cure through the use of this antibiotic. Even now, despite the plethora of antibiotics available, streptomycin remains an important medication for the treatment of tuberculosis as well as another ancient disease, plague.

As a clinician who continues to treat tuberculosis, I remain in awe of Dr. Schatz's discovery, born of such humble beginnings. While history may not afford this pioneer researcher with appropriate recognition, his contribution to humanity is immortalized by those who knew him, by those who continue to work with his antibiotic, and most importantly, by those who have experienced a restored life at the hands of his discovery.

ABOUT THE AUTHORS

Albert Schatz was born in Norwich, Connecticut, USA, in 1920, and died in Philadelphia, Pennsylvania, in January, 2005. He moved to Passaic, New Jersey, at a young age, but spent much of his childhood on his grandparents' farm in Fitchville, Connecticut.

As a 23 year old graduate student at Rutgers University in New Jersey, Schatz discovered streptomycin, the first effective drug against tuberculosis. He is known today as the co-discoverer of streptomycin.

Dr. Schatz wrote more than 700 articles, and was co-author of three textbooks. He received a multitude of medals and honors in recognition of his work in discovering streptomycin, including several gold medals from France. He was also awarded honorary degrees from Brazil, Peru, Chile and the Dominican Republic. One of his most valued awards was the Rutgers University Medal, the university's highest honor, on the occasion of the 50th anniversary of the discovery of streptomycin, in recognition of his key work in the discovery.

Inge Auerbacher was born in 1934 in Kippenheim, Germany. She was imprisoned from 1942–1945 in the Terezin concentration camp in Czechoslovakia. She emigrated to the United States in 1946, and currently lives in New York City.

Auerbacher graduated from Queens College in New York City with a B.S. degree in chemistry, and did post-graduate work in biochemistry at Hunter College. She worked for 38 years in research and clinical work, and is now retired.

Auerbacher is the author of *I am a Star—Child of the Holocaust, Beyond the Yellow Star to America,* and *Running Against the Wind.*

She is the recipient of several honors and awards, among which are the Ellis Island Medal of Honor, the Louis E. Yavner Citizen Award, and many other citations of honor from various governmental agencies. She also received an honorary Doctorate of Humane Letters from Long Island University, New York City.

Further information is available on her website, *www.ingeauerbacher.com.*

978-0-595-37997-2
0-595-37997-4

44792260R00089

Made in the USA
Middletown, DE
16 June 2017